D1582196

Pot Luck

Pot Luck

Sonia Allison

PIATKUS

© 1982 Sonia Allison

First published in 1982
by Judy Piatkus(Publishers)Limited
of Loughton, Essex

British Library Cataloguing in Publication Data

Allison, Sonia
   Pot luck.
   1. Cookery
   I. Title
   641.5'89   TX840.S/

   ISBN 0-86188-204-0

Typeset by Preface Limited, Salisbury, Wilts.
Printed and bound by R. J. Acford, Chichester.

Contents

Illustrations

Introduction

Pot Luck is a recipe book given over exclusively to casseroles and one-pot meals which can be cooked either in the oven or on the hob. Many of the recipes are perfectly suitable for slow cooking, but I would suggest that they are adapted in conjunction with the instruction book supplied with your own make of slow cooker.

The recipes range in style from simple (Golden Leek and Potato Pie) to sumptuous (Venison Braise with Feather Dumplings), and they are geared for both family eating and informal entertaining. In many instances, the dishes are complete within themselves, enabling one to cut down on preparation time, fuel and washing-up — ideal for busy, working people who resent toiling over the proverbial hot stove, and for those who are only too glad to let the cooking take care of itself. Casseroles are very adaptable and can be prepared in advance and reheated when needed, with no chance of spoiling if family or guests arrive late. Cheaper cuts of meat can be used if the cooking period is long and slow, and of course dishes can often be 'stretched' by the addition of more vegetables, pasta and pulses.

It stands to reason that not everything, every time, can be cooked together successfully. Wherever possible, I have included fresh or dried vegetables, pulses, rice, pasta, barley and other cereals with the main ingredient to make a nourishing and tasty one-pot meal, but some of the dishes do need separate accompaniments and suitable suggestions are given with each recipe.

Cookware

And now a brief word on cookware. Whenever possible, use a sturdy, heavy-based casserole or pan to ensure even heat distribution and to prevent burning and over-cooking. For pottery casseroles without lids (through breakages), cover with a double thickness of greased foil. If

9

searching out new cookware, choose the best that money can buy as it will prove a long term investment. Le Creuset flameproof dishes, in attractively-coloured enamel, last a lifetime and can be used on the hob, in the oven and for serving. But I must point out that they are heavy and not practical for those with arthritic hands and the elderly. For oven cookware, Pyrex is an old favourite and excellent choice, and so is milk-white Corning Ware which is versatile enough to be used for cooking, serving, deep freezing left-overs and reheating made-up dishes, either conventionally or in the microwave. Other makes and kinds of cookware give sound and reliable service, but choose carefully and make sure that the pot or casserole is suited to personal needs. If it is too heavy to handle, go for something lighter, selecting a different type of enamel or aluminium. If the pans are kept hanging up as a means of display, choose stainless steel and copper as these buff up to a mellow brightness with comparative ease. For rustic kitchens, oven-to-table pottery casseroles have a charm of their own and are, in general terms, economically priced. Before buying any piece of cookware for oven use, check that the handles and lid knob are heat-resistant and will neither melt nor disfigure in the heat of the oven.

To keep pans and casseroles in tip-top condition, wash and dry them thoroughly as soon as possible after use, and, when cleaning, treat coarse scouring pads and scouring powders with caution. Soak burned pans in water until the food loosens of its own accord, and avoid scraping any surface with a knife. Use metal cleaners ONLY on the outside of pans and wash thoroughly afterwards. Buff up with a soft cloth.

To make life easy, I have listed a few recipes which I especially recommend as 'complete' meals and some which are particularly good for the family, for entertaining, or simply quick to prepare.

Complete Meals

Beef
Madeira Stew
Beef à la Mode
Cholent
Beef Goulash
Family Steak and Kidney Stewpot

Lamb
Lamb Braise with Cabbage
Lamb and Gammon Casserole
Highland Lamb
Pilau of Lamb

Pork and Bacon
Westphalian Bean 'Soup'

Veal
Orchard Veal with Bacon Dumplings

Poultry and Game
Chicken Stew with Caramel Onions

Winter Chicken
Spanish Paella
Chicken Paprika Cream with Csipetke
Sweet-Sour Duck with Wine
Apple Duck with Red Cabbage

Offal
Best Liver Bake
Succulent Orange Liver

Fish
Bouillabaisse
Sweetcorn and Smoked Haddock Chowder

Vegetables, Cheese and Eggs
Dutch Vegetable Hotpot
Risotto
Ratatouille with Wine

———◆—※—◆———

Family Recipes

Beef
Crispy Beef and Vegetable Layer
Family Steak and Kidney Stewpot
Beef and Lentil Cookpot
Barley Pot with Beef Balls

Lamb
Lamb with Haricots
Lamb Cobbler

Pork and Bacon
Green Cabbage and Bacon Casserole
Farmer's Pork and Potatoe Pie
Creamy Bacon and Vegetable Bake

Poultry and Game
Spring Chicken with Apple Juice

11

Winter Chicken
Creamed Chicken with
  Corn-n-Beans

Offal
Oxtail Stew with Vegetables

Fish
Sweetcorn and Smoked Haddock
  Chowder
Smoky Fish and Bacon Cas-
  serole

Vegetables, Cheese and Eggs
Vegetable Goulash

Recipes for Entertaining

Beef
Old English Spicy Beefpot
Beef and Prune Ragout
Fruited Burgundy Beef
Brandied Beef in a Garden

Lamb
Cape Lamb 'Bredie'
Peachy Lamb Special

Pork and Bacon
Pork Layer Casserole
Bacon and Vegetable Casserole
Pork and Asparagus Layer
Pork and Beans in Cider

Veal
Martini Veal with Prunes
Hunter's Veal
Veal Chops Mozzarella

Poultry and Game
Chicken in the Swim
Grape Chicken with Almonds
Asparagus Chicken
Wine-Braised Chicken with
  Apricots
Pasta Chicken Veronique
Chicken Seville with Olive Dump-
  lings
Chicken Paprika Cream with
  Csipetke
Drunken Duck with Chestnuts
Venison Braise with Feather
  Dumplings
Peter's Orange Pheasant

Offal
Sizzling Kidneys in Red Wine
Orange Kidneys with Madeira
Succulent Orange Liver
Chicken Livers in Curry Cream
  Sauce
Ox Liver Carbonnade

Fish
Eastern Haddock

Vegetables, Cheese and Eggs
Party Rice and Lentil Curry with
  Eggs

Quick Dishes

Beef
Madeira Stew
Indian Style Beef-n-Rice

Lamb
Lamb Braise with Cabbage
Tex-Mex Lamb
Pilau of Lamb
Lamb Hotpot

Pork and Bacon
Barbecued Beans and Bangers
Rice and Sausage Hob Pot
Cumberland Sausage Casserole
Sausage Goulash
Macaroni Carbonara

Macaroni Matriciana

Poultry and Game
Barbecued Chicken
Creamed Chicken with
  Corn-n-Beans

Offal
Turkey Liver Risotto
On-the-Spot Liver Casserole

Vegetables, Cheese and Eggs
Exotic Peppers
Mushroom and Potato Braise
Hungarian Mushrooms
Brunch in a Pot

Beef

Yorkshire Stew
with Horseradish Dumplings

Appetisingly meaty, here is a splendid cold weather dish laced with port. Serve with green vegetables. (See illustration facing page 33.)

1½ oz (40 g) margarine or dripping
6 oz (175 g) onion, quartered
4 oz (125 g) carrots, sliced
3 oz (75 g) turnip, cubed
1½ lb (675 g) braising steak, cubed
14 oz (400 g) can tomatoes
12 oz (350 g) potatoes, halved or quartered, depending on size
5 tablespoons port
1 can condensed oxtail soup
½ level teaspoon mixed herbs
salt and pepper to taste

Dumplings
4 oz (125 g) self-raising flour
½ level teaspoon salt
2 oz (50 g) finely shredded suet
2 rounded teaspoons horseradish sauce
about 3 tablespoons cold milk to mix

1. Heat margarine or dripping in pan. Add onion, carrots and turnips. Cover. Fry for 15 to 20 minutes until lightly browned.
2. Remove from pan. Add meat to pan. Fry a little more briskly until well sealed and golden, then replace the vegetables.
3. Stir in tomatoes, potatoes, port, soup and herbs. Bring to boil, stirring. Season to taste. Lower heat. Cover. Simmer slowly for $1\frac{3}{4}$ hours, stirring from time to time.
4. To make dumplings, sift flour and salt into bowl. Toss in suet. Mix to soft dough with horseradish sauce and milk.
5. Shape into 8 dumplings. After $1\frac{3}{4}$ hours, drop gently on top of stew. Cover. Simmer for a further 20 to 25 minutes or until well puffed and cooked through. Spoon on to warm plates.

Serves 6

Old English Spicy Beefpot

Mellowed with ale and brimming with herbs and spices, this is a lovely, welcoming dish for any time of year.

2 lb (900 g) braising steak
2 oz (50 g) flour
2 level teaspoons mustard powder
1 level teaspoon salt
1½ oz (40 g) butter or margarine
8 oz (225 g) onions, chopped
2 level tablespoons tomato purée
2 level tablespoons paprika
¼ level teaspoon cayenne pepper
1 level teaspoon thyme
1 pint (575 ml) ale
1 lb (450 g) potatoes, halved or quartered, depending on size
4 oz (125 g) button mushrooms
2 heaped tablespoons chopped parsley or chopped fresh dill

1. Wash and dry steak and cut into cubes. Coat with flour, first mixed with mustard and salt.
2. Heat butter or margarine in pan. Add meat and onions. Fry over medium heat until both are golden brown. Tip any left over flour mixture into pan.
3. Stir in purée, paprika, cayenne pepper, thyme and ale. Bring to boil, stirring. Cover. Simmer for 1½ hours. Add potatoes. Cover again and continue to cook for a further 20 minutes.
4. Mix in mushrooms. Cook for another 15 to 20 minutes. Transfer to serving dish and sprinkle with parsley or dill.

Serves 6

Old English Spicy Porkpot
Make exactly as the previous recipe but use diced stewing pork instead of beef.

17

Beef and Prune Ragout

Rich and fruity, a special occasion main course with a subtle flavouring of red wine. Serve with plain boiled potatoes or rice.

1½ lb (675 g) braising steak
2 oz (50 g) flour
1½ oz (40 g) butter or margarine
2 teaspoons salad oil
4 oz (125 g) onions, chopped
1 garlic clove, crushed
1 tablespoon Worcestershire sauce
¼ pint (150 ml) beef stock
¼ pint (150 ml) dry red wine
1 rounded tablespoon tomato chutney
2 medium celery stalks, sliced
4 oz (125 g) carrots, sliced
finely grated peel and juice of 1 medium orange
1 level teaspoon mixed herbs
4 oz (125 g) stoned prunes, soaked overnight
2 level teaspoons salt
15 oz (425 g) can red kidney beans, drained and rinsed

1. Cube beef and coat with flour. Heat butter or margarine and oil in pan. Add beef, onions and garlic. Fry fairly briskly until well browned.
2. Stir in Worcestershire sauce, stock, wine and chutney. Bring to boil, stirring. Add celery, carrots, orange peel and juice, herbs, drained prunes and salt.
3. Lower heat. Cover. Simmer for 2 hours or until beef is tender, stirring occasionally. Mix in beans. Heat through for another 7 to 10 minutes, stirring.

Serves 4

Fruited Steak and Kidney Ragout
Make exactly as the previous recipe, but use 1 lb (450 g) braising steak and 8 oz (225 g) ox kidney.

Family Steak and Kidney Stewpot

A popular combination which, with the whole potatoes added towards the end, makes a traditional all-in-one dish for cold-weather eating. Serve with wedges of cooked cabbage. (See illustration facing page 32.)

> *1 lb (450 g) chuck steak*
> *4 to 6 lambs' kidneys*
> *1 oz (25 g) flour mixed with 2 rounded teaspoons mustard powder*
>   *and 2 level teaspoons salt*
> *2 oz (50 g) margarine or dripping*
> *6 oz (175 g) onions, chopped*
> *2 small swedes, quartered*
> *4 small carrots, quartered*
> *½ pint (275 ml) beef stock*
> *1 heaped tablespoon chopped parsley*
> *4 oz (125 g) trimmed mushrooms, sliced*
> *1 lb (450 g) potatoes, quartered*

1. Wash and dry steak. Cut into 1 inch (2½ cm) cubes. Peel kidneys then halve, core and dice. Toss both steak and kidney in flour mixture until all the pieces are well coated.
2. Heat margarine or dripping in pan. Add onions. Fry until pale gold. Add beef and kidney cubes. Fry, turning, until well sealed and brown.
3. Mix in swedes and carrots. Pour stock into pan then add parsley. Bring to boil, stirring. Lower heat and cover. Simmer for 1½ hours or until beef is just tender.
4. Stir in mushrooms. Arrange potatoes on top of meat mixture. Cover. Continue to cook for a further 20 to 25 minutes or until potatoes are soft.

Serves 4

Crispy Beef and Vegetable Layer

A fairly economical dish, with an unusual topping of potato crisps.

1 oz (25 g) butter or margarine
4 oz (125 g) onions, grated
1 lb (450 g) lean minced raw beef
2 level teaspoons mixed herbs
1 lb (450 g) potatoes, grated
8 oz (225 g) carrots, grated
2 oz (50 g) swede, grated
2 heaped tablespoons finely chopped parsley
2 level teaspoons salt
pepper to taste
½ pint (275 ml) boiling water
5 heaped tablespoons crushed potato crisps

1. Heat butter or margarine in pan. Add onions and beef. Fry for about 20 minutes over medium heat until both are golden brown, fork-stirring often to crumble meat and stop it forming a solid lump.
2. Meanwhile, mix together the herbs, potatoes, carrots, swede and parsley. Fill a well-greated casserole with alternate layers of mince and vegetable mixtures.
3. End with vegetables and sprinkle salt and pepper between layers. Carefully pour water into dish then sprinkle top with crisps. Bake uncovered for 1 hour in moderate oven set to 180°C (350°F), Gas 4.

Serves 4

Crispy Pork and Vegetable Layer
Follow previous recipe but use minced stewing pork instead of beef.

Beef and Lentil Cookpot

A handy, warming beef dish with Oriental overtones. Serve with rice.

1 tablespoon salad oil
8 oz (225 g) onions, chopped
2 lb (900 g) braising steak
8 oz (225 g) red lentils
1 lb (450 g) white cabbage, shredded
2 rounded teaspoons mild curry powder
1 pint (575 ml) boiling water
8 oz (225 g) frozen or canned sweetcorn
1 to 2 rounded teaspoons salt

1. Heat oil in large pan until sizzling. Add onions and fry until golden. Remove from pan.
2. Add beef to pan. Fry briskly until well-browned and sealed.
3. Stir in the onions and all remaining ingredients. Mix well. Bring to boil, stirring.
4. Lower heat. Cover. Simmer very gently until meat is tender, allowing about $1\frac{3}{4}$ to 2 hours. Top up with extra boiling water if gravy seems to be thickening up too much. Serve piping hot.

Serves 6 to 8

Piquant Beef
with Herb Dumplings

An easy-to-make beef dish. Bake potatoes alongside the casserole and also serve seasonal green vegetables.

2 oz (50 g) butter or margarine
12 oz (350 g) frozen macedoine of vegetables (no need to thaw)
2 lb (900 g) braising steak, diced
1 level tablespoon cornflour
8 oz (225 g) can baked beans in tomato sauce
1 level teaspoon salt
2 level teaspoons onion salt
4 tablespoons malt vinegar
1 level teaspoon mixed spice
¾ pint (425 ml) water

Dumplings
8 oz (225 g) self-raising flour
½ level teaspoon salt
1 oz (25 g) butter or margarine
1 level teaspoon dried thyme
¼ pint (150 ml) cold milk

1. Heat butter or margarine in large, wide pan. Add vegetables. Sizzle over medium heat for about 15 minutes or until golden brown. Stir occasionally. Remove to plate.
2. Put steak into pan, a few pieces at a time, and fry over fairly brisk heat until well-browned and sealed. Stir in vegetables, cornflour, beans, salt, onion salt, vinegar, spice and water.
3. Bring to boil, stirring. Lower heat and cover. Simmer gently for 1½ to 2 hours or until tender. Stir occasionally to prevent sticking.
4. To make dumplings, sift flour and salt into bowl. Rub in margarine. Toss in thyme, then, using a fork, mix to a soft dough with milk, adding it all at once. Shape into 12 dumplings with floured hands and drop on top of stew.
5. Cover with lid and continue to simmer for a further 15 to 20 minutes or until dumplings are well-puffed and at least twice their original size. Serve piping hot.

Serves 6

22

Fruited Burgundy Beef

A flamboyant hotpot packed with delicious ingredients and sufficiently haute cuisine to please the most discerning of guests! Serve with boiled potatoes and a green salad.

1 oz (25 g) butter or margarine
1 tablespoon salad oil
2 garlic cloves, crushed
8 oz (225 g) onions, chopped
1½ lb (675 g) braising steak, cubed
1 tablespoon Worcestershire sauce
½ pint (275 ml) red Burgundy
3 oz (75 g) dried apricots, soaked overnight
finely grated peel and juice of 1 medium orange
2 level tablespoons tomato purée
2 large celery stalks, sliced
6 oz (175 g) carrots, sliced
4 oz (125 g) parsnips, diced
1 bouquet garni
2 rounded tablespoons light brown soft sugar
2 to 3 level teaspoons salt
2 level tablespoons cornflour
3 tablespoons cold water

1. Melt butter or margarine in flameproof casserole. Add oil. Heat until sizzling. Add crushed garlic and onions. Fry until pale gold.
2. Add beef cubes a few pieces at a time. Fry until well sealed and browned. Stir in remaining ingredients except cornflour and water.
3. Mix well. Bring to boil, stirring. Lower heat. Cover closely with lid or greased foil. Transfer to cool oven set to 160°C (325°F), Gas 3.
4. Cook for 2½ to 3 hours, when meat should be tender. Remove from oven and stand over low heat on hob.
5. Mix cornflour smoothly with water and add to beef mixture. Cook, stirring, until bubbling and thickened. Remove bouquet garni and discard. Simmer beef for a further 5 minutes before serving.

Serves 4 to 6

Brandied Beef in a Garden

Very much a special occasion dish, made with a piece of beef topside, a myriad of vegetables and a generous splash of brandy. Serve with a salad or green vegetables.

3 lb (1½ kg) topside
3 level tablespoons flour
2 oz (50 g) butter or margarine
8 oz (225 g) onions, chopped
8 oz (225 g) carrots, sliced
4 oz (125 g) swede, diced
4 oz (125 g) parsnip, diced
4 oz (125 g) Jerusalem artichokes, sliced
3 large celery stalks, sliced
1 lb (450 g) potatoes, grated
¾ pint (425 ml) beef stock
2 level teaspoons salt
1 bouquet garni
1 level teaspoon finely grated orange peel
4 tablespoons brandy

1. Wash and dry beef and coat all over with flour. Heat butter or margarine in heavy pan. Add beef. Fry until well browned all over. Remove to plate.
2. Add all prepared vegetables, except potatoes, to remaining fat in pan. Fry for about 15 minutes over medium heat or until vegetables are pale gold. Stir from time to time.
3. Mix in potatoes, beef stock, salt, bouquet garni and grated orange peel. Bring to boil, stirring. Replace beef. Cover pan and simmer over lowest possible heat for between 2½ to 3 hours or until meat is tender. Stir occasionally to prevent sticking.
4. Remove beef to carving board and slice. Take bouquet garni out of pan and discard. Warm the brandy in separate pan, ignite then add to vegetable and pan juices. Stir until flames have subsided then transfer to serving dish. Place slices of meat on top and serve hot.

Serves 6

Bulgarian Meat Balls in Yogurt

An unusual but delicious main course which is reasonably budget-minded.

1½ lb (675 g) raw minced beef
2 Grade 3 eggs
2 oz (50 g) fresh white breadcrumbs
2 level teaspoons oregano or marjoram
3 oz (75 g) onions, grated
1 garlic clove, crushed
2 level teaspoons salt
white pepper to taste
1 pint (575 ml) boiling beef stock
4 oz (125 g) easy-cook long grain rice
5 oz (150 g) natural yogurt
2 Grade 3 egg yolks
2 tablespoons cold water
chopped fresh mint or parsley for garnishing

1. Mix beef with eggs, breadcrumbs, oregano or marjoram, onions, garlic, salt and pepper. With wet hands, shape into small balls about the size of an apricot.
2. Pour stock into large pan. Add rice and meat balls. Bring to boil, stirring gently. Lower heat. Cover.
3. Simmer gently for 30 minutes. Beat yogurt with egg yolks and water. Pour into pan and mix in well.
4. Remove from heat and transfer to serving dish. Sprinkle with mint or parsley.

Serves 6

Curly-Topped Beef Pie

Easy to make, this two-part meat dish ends up tasty and troublefree!

1 lb (450 g) raw minced beef
4 oz (125 g) onion, grated
4 oz (125 g) carrots, grated
1 level tablespoon brown ketchup
2 level teaspoons salt
1 level tablespoon creamed horseradish
1 teaspoon Worcestershire sauce
½ pint (275 ml) dry red wine
1 level tablespoon cornflour
2 tablespoons cold water
1 lb (450 g) cold boiled potatoes
1 oz (25 g) butter or margarine, melted
1 level teaspoon paprika

1. Put beef into pan with onions, carrots, ketchup, salt, creamed horseradish, Worcestershire sauce and wine. Bring to boil, breaking up meat with a fork all the time.
2. Lower heat. Cover. Simmer gently for 1 hour. To thicken, blend cornflour smoothly with water. Add to beef. Bring to boil, stirring.
3. Spoon hot beef mixture into 2½-pint (1½-litre) greased heatproof dish. Grate potatoes over top then coat with melted butter or margarine. Sprinkle with paprika and brown under a hot grill.

Serves 4 to 6

Barley Pot with Beef Balls

Simple and unpretentious but quite delicious and wonderfully warming in the winter.

3 oz (75 g) pearl barley
1 pint (575 ml) boiling water
2 large leeks, sliced
1 level teaspoon salt

Beef Balls
1 lb (450 g) raw lean minced beef
2 level teaspoons fine semolina
1 level teaspoon onion salt
1 Grade 2 egg, beaten

1. Tip washed barley into heavy saucepan. Add water, leeks and salt. Bring to boil. Lower heat. Cover. Simmer for 45 minutes.
2. Meanwhile, knead beef with semolina, onion salt and egg.
3. Shape into 8 balls with damp hands and arrange on top of barley. Cover and simmer for a further 45 minutes.

Serves 4

Beef Stuffed Peppers

Tasty and filling, I always make these when peppers are plentiful and use either, red, green or yellow—or even a mixture of peppers for fun! They are very undemanding of time or attention and taste good either hot with rice or cold.

> *4 large peppers (1½ lb or 675 g)*
> *1 lb (450 g) lean minced beef*
> *3 oz (75 g) easy-cook long grain rice*
> *6 oz (175 g) onions, grated*
> *2 level teaspoons salt*
> *¼ pint (150 ml) water*
> *½ pint (275 ml) tomato juice*

1. Wash and dry peppers. Cut off tops and set aside for lids. Remove inside fibres and seeds from each and discard. If necessary, cut very thin slivers off the bases of peppers so that they stand upright without toppling.
2. Mix together beef, rice, onion, salt and water. Pack equal amounts into peppers and stand upright, and close together, in saucepan. Top with reserved lids.
3. Pour tomato juice into pan. Bring to boil then cover. Simmer gently for 1 hour. Allow 1 pepper per person and coat with pan juices.

Serves 4

Middle Eastern Stuffed Peppers

Follow previous recipe but use 1 lb (450 g) lean minced raw lamb (cut from leg) instead of beef. Include 1 oz (25 g) pine nuts and 1 oz (25 g) seedless raisins in addition to the rice, onion and salt.

Madeira Stew

A chunky, simple stew, popular on the sub-tropical island of Madeira.

1 lb (450 g) braising steak
1 tablespoon salad oil
4 oz (125 g) onions, coarsely grated
1 garlic clove, sliced
4 oz (125 g) carrots, thickly sliced
1 rounded tablespoon tomato purée
½ level teaspoon continental mustard
½ pint (275 ml) Madeira
1 to 1½ level teaspoons salt
¼ pint (150 ml) water
6 oz (175 g) pasta shells or bows

1. Cut steak into cubes. Heat oil in pan. Add onions, garlic, carrots and beef cubes. Fry over medium heat for about 10 minutes or until golden brown, turning fairly frequently.
2. Stir in purée, mustard, Madeira, salt and water. Bring to boil. Cover. Lower heat. Simmer for 1½ hours or until meat is just tender.
3. Add pasta. Mix in well. Continue to simmer for a further 20 to 25 minutes or until cooked.

Serves 4

Borsch

The ultimate in fine soups, Russian Borsch also makes a stunning main course, served in deep plates with freshly boiled potatoes and rye bread.

1½ lb (675 g) beef shin, cut into strips
3½ pints (2 litres) cold water
3 level teaspoons salt
1 lb (450 g) raw beetroots, grated
12 oz (350 g) onions, chopped
2 large trimmed leeks, sliced
4 oz (125 g) carrots, sliced
4 oz (125 g) turnip, cubed
4 oz (125 g) parsnip, cubed
4 oz (125 g) swede, cubed
1 lb (450 g) white cabbage, shredded
2 oz (50 g) tomato purée
6 oz (175 g) cooked beetroots, grated
2 tablespoons lemon juice
1 level tablespoon brown sugar
5 oz (142 ml) carton soured cream.

1. Put beef into large pan with water, salt, raw beets, onions, leeks, carrots, turnip, parsnip, swede, cabbage and purée.
2. Bring to boil, stirring. Lower heat. Cover. Simmer for about 2 hours or until meat is really tender, stirring occasionally. Mix in cooked beetroots (which will turn Borsch bright red), lemon juice and sugar.
3. Reheat for 5 to 7 minutes then ladle into deep plates. Top each with dollops of soured cream.

Serves 6 to 8

Beef à la Mode

An accommodating dish which I have adapted slightly from the classic French version, adding more vegetables to make a complete meal.

> 3 lb (1½ kg) chuck steak, in one piece
> 3 level tablespoons flour
> 2 oz (50 g) butter or margarine
> 3 teaspoons salad oil
> ¾ pint (425 ml) dry red wine
> 1 bouquet garni
> 1 lb (450 g) carrots, each cut lengthwise into 4 pieces
> 12 oz (350 g) shallots or small onions
> 2 level teaspoons salt
> 1 lb (450 g) potatoes, halved or quartered, depending on size
> 8 oz (225 g) button mushrooms
> 4 tablespoons brandy

1. Wash and dry steak. Coat all over with flour. Heat butter or margarine and oil in large pan. Add steak. Fry until well browned, turning several times with two spoons. (Do not use a fork as it will pierce meat and cause all the juice to escape.)
2. Add wine and bouquet garni. Bring slowly to boil. Cover. Simmer for 2 hours over minimal heat.
3. Add carrots, shallots and salt. Cover and continue to simmer for a further 30 minutes. Add potatoes. Cook, still covered, until tender, allowing about 25 to 30 minutes.
4. Remove meat to board and carve into slices. Take bouquet garni out of pan and discard. Return meat to pan. Add mushrooms and reheat, stirring, for about 10 minutes.
5. Warm brandy in a separate pan and flame. Add to beef mixture. Stir in well.

Serves 6 to 8

31

Cholent

A Jewish dish, still made by members of the orthodox community as, in theory, it requires no preparation on the Sabbath and is cooked the day before. On a more practical basis, Cholent is a close relation of Spain's Cocido and can be satisfactorily prepared and cooked in about 9 hours—perfect for Aga cookers!

12 oz (350 g) butter beans, soaked overnight
3 lb (1½ kg) top rib of beef or unsalted rolled brisket
12 oz (425 g) marrow bone, left whole (optional)
1 lb (450 g) onions, quartered
2 lb (900 g) potatoes, quartered
2 level teaspoons salt
1½ pints (⅞ litre) water

1. Put beans into deep casserole. Place meat and marrow bone, if used, on top.
2. Surround with vegetables then sprinkle with salt. Pour water into dish.
3. Cover very securely. Cook for 8 to 9 hours in very slow oven set to 110°C (225°F), Gas ¼.
4. Remove from oven, skim off fat then lift out meat on to board. Cut into portions and serve with the beans, vegetables and gravy.

Serves 8

Right: Family Steak and Kidney Stewpot (page 19).

Chili Con Carne (1)

A Mexican style dish which has achieved world-wide popularity over the last ten years or so. I use Schwarz chili seasoning for flavouring as it is a well-balanced, mahogany-coloured blend with its own subtle and distinctive taste, and especially suited to this type of cooking. But there is nothing to stop you, if preferred, from using cayenne pepper or Tabasco for 'hotting-up' the Chili. Serve with rice.

$1\frac{1}{2}$ tablespoons salad oil
4 oz (125 g) onion, chopped
4 oz (125 g) green pepper, cut into strips
1 lb (450 g) raw minced beef
2 oz (50 g) tomato purée
1 garlic clove, crushed (optional)
15 oz (425 g) can baked beans in tomato sauce
3 rounded teaspoons Schwarz chili seasoning or 1 to 2 level teas-
    poons cayenne pepper or Tabasco
$\frac{1}{2}$ to 1 level teaspoon salt
$\frac{1}{4}$ pint (150 ml) tomato juice
1 level teaspoon dark brown sugar

1. Heat oil in sturdy pan. Add onions and pepper and fry gently until onions are golden, allowing about 10 to 12 minutes. Remove from pan.
2. Add beef and stir-fry until crumbly and well browned. Mix in fried onions, purée, garlic, beans in sauce, chili seasoning (or cayenne pepper or Tabasco), salt, tomato juice and sugar.
3. Bring to boil, stirring. Lower heat and cover. Simmer gently for 45 minutes, stirring from time to time to prevent sticking.

Serves 4

Left: Yorkshire Stew with Horseradish Dumplings (page 16).

33

Chili Con Carne (2)

A more traditional version using red kidney beans which can be put together in minutes and left to cook happily by itself. Serve with ready-prepared and packeted Tortillas which are available from major supermarkets and food stores for an authentic accompaniment.

1 lb (450 g) raw minced beef
½ packet (just over ½ oz or 15 g) dried sliced onion
¼ packet (just over ¼ oz or 8 g) dried red and green pepper flakes
14 oz (400 g) can tomatoes
1 garlic clove, crushed
1 to 1½ level teaspoons chili powder
1 lb (450 g) can red kidney beans, drained
½ pint (275 ml) tomato juice
1 level teaspoon salt
4 oz (125 g) Cheddar cheese, grated

1. Put meat into pan and stir over medium heat until crumbly and well-browned.
2. Mix in onion and pepper flakes, the tomatoes, garlic, chili powder, beans, tomato juice and salt. Bring to boil, stirring.
3. Lower heat. Cover. Simmer for 45 minutes, stirring frequently to prevent sticking. To serve, spoon on to plates and sprinkle with cheese.

Serves 4

Indian Style Beef-n-Rice

Good to make when you are in a hurry and want a dish to please all the family. Serve with natural yogurt, a mixed salad and chutney.

1 lb (450 g) raw minced beef
1 garlic clove, crushed
1 small red or green pepper, coarsely chopped
8 oz (225 g) easy-cook Indian Basmati rice
1 pint (575 ml) beef stock
2 level teaspoons salt
2 level teaspoons turmeric (to give rice yellow colour)

1. Fry meat and garlic over medium heat until well browned and crumbly, fork-stirring all the time.
2. Add rest of ingredients and mix in well. Bring to boil. Lower heat. Cover. Simmer for 30 minutes or until rice grains are separate and fluffy and have absorbed all the stock.
3. Serve very hot.

Serves 4

Sauerbraten

Here is a world famous, old-time sweet-sour classic. It should be eaten with boiled potatoes and hot sauerkraut.

3½ lbs (1½ kg) lean braising steak, in one piece and washed

Marinade
¼ pint (125 ml) malt vinegar
½ pint (275 ml) water
8 oz (225 g) onions, thinly sliced
1 large celery stalk, thickly sliced
1 large bay leaf, crumbled
1 bouquet garni bag, opened out
about 1 level teaspoon coarsely milled black pepper
½ teaspoon Tabasco

To cook
2 oz (50 g) margarine
4 oz (125 g) streaky bacon, chopped
6 oz (175 g) onions, chopped
4 oz (125 g) tomatoes, blanched, skinned and chopped
2 oz (50 g) ginger snaps, broken into small pieces
1 level tablespoon each tomato purée and cornflour
2 tablespoons cold water
salt and pepper

1. Put beef into glass or enamel bowl. Mix marinade and pour over meat. Cover with cling film. Refrigerate 3 days, turning daily.
2. To cook, melt margarine in pan. Add bacon and onions. Fry gently until gold. Move to one side. Add beef. Fry briskly until browned.
3. Add marinade, tomatoes, ginger snaps and purée. Bring to boil, stirring. Cover. Simmer very gently for 2 to 2 ½ hours.
4. Lift meat on to board and keep hot. Sieve sauce into clean saucepan. Reheat then stir in cornflour mixed smoothly with water. Bring to boil, stirring. Simmer for 2 minutes. If necessary, thin down with water or, for a sourer flavour, with vinegar.
5. Carve meat and arrange on hot dish. Coat with sauce and serve.

Serves 8

Spanish Stew

A rich and warmly filling stew, packed with flavour and with an addition common to both the Spanish and Portuguese—chick peas.

2 tablespoons salad oil
8 oz (225 g) onions, chopped
8 oz (225 g) carrots, thinly sliced
4 large celery stalks, sliced
1 medium leek, with 2 inches (5 cm) green 'skirt' left on
6 oz (175 g) piece of garlic sausage, skinned and diced
8 oz (225 g) lean bacon, de-rinded and diced
1½ lb (675 g) chuck steak, diced
1 bottle Spanish Rioja wine
1 level teaspoon salt
1 lb (450 g) potatoes, cut into large cubes
14 oz (400 g) can chick peas, drained
1 level tablespoon cornflour
2 tablespoons cold water
pepper to taste

1. Heat oil in large pan. Add onions, carrots and celery. Fry gently for 5 minutes. Wash leek thoroughly and shred. Add to pan with sausage and bacon. Continue to fry for a further 10 minutes or until ingredients turn a warm shade of gold. Remove to one side of pan.
2. Add beef, a few pieces at a time. Fry until brown and well sealed.
3. Pour wine into pan. Add salt. Bring to boil. Lower heat. Cover. Simmer for 1½ hours. Add potatoes. Cook for a further 20 minutes.
4. Mix in chick peas. To thicken, blend cornflour smoothly with water. Pour into pan. Cook, stirring, until stew comes to boil and thickens. Season with pepper. Simmer for further 5 minutes. Serve very hot.

Serves 6

Beef Goulash

A colourful, classic Hungarian dish which is hearty, wholesome and filling. The addition of macaroni and potatoes at the end makes the goulash a complete meal with no extras needed. (See jacket picture.)

2 oz (50 g) lard, white cooking fat or margarine
12 oz (350 g) onions, chopped
2 medium green peppers, cut into fine strips
2 garlic cloves, chopped
2 lb (900 g) braising steak, diced
1 level teaspoon caraway seeds
2 level tablespoons paprika
1½ level teaspoons salt
6 canned tomatoes, chopped
2 oz (50 g) elbow or other short macaroni
1 lb (450 g) potatoes, cut into large cubes
¼ pint (150 ml) water

1. Heat fat in heavy pan. Add onions and fry for 10 minutes over moderate heat until light gold. Add peppers and garlic. Continue to fry for a further 7 minutes, stirring occasionally.
2. Add steak, a few pieces at a time, and fry briskly until brown and well sealed.
3. Stir in caraway seeds, paprika, salt and tomatoes. Bring to boil, stirring. Cover. Cook very gently for 2 hours (no extra liquid needed as vegetables and meat produce enough), stirring once or twice.
4. Mix in macaroni, stand potatoes on top then cover with the lid. Continue to simmer for a further 25 to 30 minutes.
5. Spoon on to warm plates and, if liked, add a dollop of soured cream or yogurt to each.

Serves 6 to 8

Cabbage Football

An economical and appetising dish, well suited to mid-week eating. Serve with jacket or roast potatoes.

2 lb (1 kg) savoy cabbage
1 lb (450 g) raw minced beef
2 oz (50 g) fresh white breadcrumbs
4 oz (125 g) onion, grated
1 level teaspoon salt
½ level teaspoon mustard powder
1 Grade 3 egg
1¼ pint (700 ml) stock (use cubes or Marmite and water)

1. Remove outer leaves from cabbage. Discard any that are damaged. Wash remainder. Keep on one side for time being.
2. Cut a slice off top of cabbage. Scoop out inside, leaving a 1-inch (2½-cm) thick shell. Shred finely then shred the slice from top and outside leaves.
3. Arrange shredded cabbage in deep heatproof dish. Mix beef thoroughly with all remaining ingredients except the stock.
4. Press into hollowed out cabbage then coat with the stock. Cover with greased lid or double thickness of greased foil.
5. Cook for 1½ hours in oven set to 180°C (350°F), Gas 4. Cut into 6 portions and serve while still very hot.

Serves 6

Rice and Sausage Hob Pot

A short-cut on-the-hob cookup, using convenience ingredients.

1 oz (25 g) dripping, lard or margarine
1 lb (450 g) beef sausages
4 oz (125 g) onions, chopped
8 oz (225 g) easy-cook long grain rice
8 oz (225 g) tomatoes, blanched, skinned and chopped
8 oz (225 g) canned or frozen sweetcorn, thawed.
1 pint (575 ml) beef stock

1. Heat dripping, lard or margarine in pan. Add sausages and onions. Fry until both are golden brown all over, turning from time to time. Keep heat fairly low and allow about 15 to 20 minutes.
2. Add all remaining ingredients. Bring to boil, stirring. Cover.
3. Lower heat. Simmer for 20 to 25 minutes or until rice grains are separate and fluffy and have absorbed all the liquid.

Serves 4

Rice and Gammon Hob Pot
Make as above but substitute 12 oz (350 g) diced raw gammon for the sausages.

Rice and Chicken Liver Hob Pot
Make exactly as above, substituting 12 oz (350 g) washed and dried chicken livers for the sausages.

Lamb

Lamb Braise with Cabbage

A delicious idea from New Zealand which is popular with those who dislike onions in cooking! It is also fast to prepare. (See illustration facing page 64).

1 tablespoon salad oil
4 New Zealand lamb leg bone steaks
8 oz (225 g) white cabbage, finely shredded
½ pint (275 ml) chicken stock
2 level teaspoons prepared English mustard
½ to 1 level teaspoon salt
1 level teaspoon paprika
12 oz (350 g) potatoes, halved or quartered, depending on size
5 oz (142 ml) carton soured cream

Garnish
4 oz (125 g) mushrooms, sliced and fried

1. Heat oil in pan. Add lamb steaks. Fry until golden brown on both sides, turning twice.
2. Add cabbage, stock, mustard, salt, paprika and potatoes. Bring to boil, stirring. Lower heat. Cover.
3. Simmer for 40 minutes then stir in soured cream. Turn into a warm dish and sprinkle with mushrooms.

Serves 4

Scotch Lamb with Apricots

This recipe is quite different from anything I have ever tasted before. It is intriguingly flavoured with canned apricots, and is just right for a cold winter night.

2½ lb (1 kg) lamb shoulder
1 oz (25 g) butter or margarine
1 level tablespoon flour
8 oz (225 g) can drained apricots, blended to purée
½ pint (275 ml) milk
1 level teaspoon paprika
3 oz (75 g) green pepper, chopped
salt and pepper
1½ lb (675 g) potatoes, very thinly sliced

1. Bone lamb, trim away surplus fat and cut meat into small cubes. Heat butter or margarine in pan. Add lamb. Fry until well sealed and brown, turning. Remove to plate.
2. Stir flour into pan. Gradually blend in apricot purée and milk. Cook, stirring, until mixture comes to boil and thickens.
3. Add paprika and green pepper then season to taste with salt and pepper. Stir in lamb cubes and arrange half the mixture over base of well-greased, medium-sized casserole.
4. Cover with half the potatoes, then top with rest of lamb mixture and finish with a layer of potatoes.
5. Cover with lid or greased foil and bake for 2 hours in a moderate oven set to 180°C (350°F), Gas 4. Uncover and continue to cook for a further 30 minutes until potatoes are brown.

Serves 4 to 5

Summer Lamb

An extravaganza of lamb and summer vegetables which makes a memorable feast.

1½ lb (675 g) neck of lamb fillet
1 oz (25 g) butter or margarine
1 lb (450 g) tomatoes, blanched, skinned and chopped
½ pint (275 ml) water
1 teaspoon Worcestershire sauce
1 level teaspoon soft brown sugar
1 level teaspoon finely chopped fresh mint
12 shallots or small onions, left whole
8 oz (225 g) fresh runner beans, sliced
6 oz (175 g) fresh peas, shelled
12 new potatoes
2 level teaspoons salt
2 level tablespoons cornflour
3 tablespoons cold water

1. Cut fillet of lamb into 1-inch (2½-cm) thick pieces. Heat butter or margarine in pan. Add lamb. Fry briskly until well sealed and golden.
2. Mix in tomatoes then add water, Worcestershire sauce, sugar and mint. Bring to boil, stirring. Cover. Simmer for 45 minutes.
3. Add remaining vegetables with salt. Cover. Simmer for a further 30 to 45 minutes or until both the meat and vegetables are tender.
4. To thicken, mix cornflour smoothly with water. Add to meat and bring to boil, stirring. Simmer for 5 minutes.

Serves 4 to 6

Summer Veal
Make as Summer Lamb but use diced pie veal instead of lamb.

44

Balkan Lamb and Vegetable Stew

Colourful and immensely tasty, this is another dish well-suited to summer. If liked, serve with a green salad.

2 oz (50 g) sunflower or other salad oil
1½ lb (675 g) leg of lamb, boned and cut into small dice
14 oz (400 g) can tomatoes or the equivalent amount of fresh tomatoes, blanched, skinned and chopped
8 oz (225 g) onions, coarsely grated
2 level teaspoons marjoram
2 level teaspoons salt
½ level teaspoon cayenne pepper or Tabasco (fiery so omit if preferred)
½ pint (250 ml) hot chicken stock
1 lb (450 g) new potatoes
1 level teaspoon cornflour
2 tablespoons cold water
5 oz (150 g) natural yogurt
1 Grade 2 egg yolk
1 level tablespoon finely chopped parsley for garnish

1. Heat oil in large pan. Add lamb. Fry fairly briskly until well sealed. Add tomatoes, onions, marjoram, salt, cayenne pepper or Tabasco and chicken stock.
2. Bring to boil. Lower heat. Cover. Simmer for about 1½ hours or until lamb is just tender. Add potatoes. Continue to simmer, covered, for a further 25 to 30 minutes or until cooked.
3. To thicken, blend cornflour with water. Beat in yogurt and egg yolk. Pour into pan. Cook, stirring gently, until mixture comes to boil and thickens. Remove from heat and leave to stand for 5 minutes.
4. Transfer to warm serving dish and sprinkle with parsley.

Serves 4

Cape Lamb `Bredie´

This traditional, Dutch-inspired lamb stew comes from South Africa. It is flavoured with curry powder and enhanced further by the addition of toasted almonds, currants and red wine. It is perfect for entertaining and sufficiently off-beat to arouse interest. Serve with plain boiled rice.

4 lb (2 kg) leg of lamb
½ bottle red wine
2 garlic cloves, crushed
2 level teaspoons salt
1 lb (450 g) firm tomatoes, blanched, skinned and chopped
1 level teaspoon dried thyme
2 level tablespoons cornflour
2 tablespoons cold water
1 rounded tablespoon dark brown soft sugar
2 level tablespoons Madras curry powder
2 oz (50 g) flaked and toasted almonds
2 oz (50 g) currants
pepper

1. Wash and dry lamb then remove as much excess fat as possible. Place in large pan with wine. Add garlic, salt, tomatoes and thyme.
2. Bring to boil. Lower heat. Cover. Simmer for 2 to 2½ hours or until lamb is tender. Remove joint from pan and carve into thick slices. Arrange on a warm oblong serving dish.
3. Mix cornflour smoothly with water then stir into pan juices to thicken. Bring to boil, stirring. Simmer for 5 minutes.
4. Add all remaining ingredients and simmer for 7 minutes. Coat lamb slices with the 'Bredie' sauce. Serve immediately.

Serves 8

Middle Eastern Lamb with Okra

For those who like the somewhat exotic combination of lamb, okra (also called ladies' fingers) and rice, this Middle Eastern speciality will make a welcome change.

12 oz (350 g) okra
1½ oz (40 g) butter or margarine
2 teaspoons salad oil
1 lb (450 g) boned leg of lamb, finely minced
4 oz (125 g) onions, chopped
1 garlic clove, crushed
6 oz (175 g) easy-cook long grain rice
8 oz (225 g) tomatoes, blanched, skinned and chopped
2 rounded tablespoons tomato purée
2 rounded tablespoons seedless raisins
½ oz (15 g) pine nuts
1 pint (575 ml) chicken stock
2 level teaspoons salt
lemon wedges for garnish

1. Top and tail okra then wash thoroughly and wipe dry. Heat half the butter or margarine and all the oil in a large pan. Add okra. Fry gently for 20 minutes, turning with 2 spoons. Remove to plate.
2. Add rest of butter or margarine to pan and melt. Mix in minced lamb, onions and garlic. Fry for 20 minutes over medium heat until well browned, fork-stirring frequently.
3. Add all remaining ingredients then replace okra. Mix well. Transfer to 3-pint (1¾-litre) greased heatproof dish.
4. Cover with lid or foil. Cook for 1 hour in moderately hot oven set to 200°C (400°F), Gas 6. Garnish with 4 or 6 wedges of lemon.

Serves 4 to 5

Highland Lamb

Something I cooked up many years ago and have been making ever since because, as a family, we all love savoury dishes with oats.

> *2 lb (900 g) neck of lamb, divided into neat pieces*
> *1 oz (25 g) flour*
> *1½ oz (40 g) margarine or dripping*
> *8 oz (225 g) white cabbage, coarsely shredded*
> *1 oz (25 g) oats*
> *14 oz (400 g) can tomatoes*
> *½ pint (275 ml) boiling water*
> *1 large leek, 3 inches (7½ cm) green 'skirt' left, and shredded*
> *2 level teaspoons salt*
> *½ level teaspoon finely grated lemon peel*
> *1 lb (450 g) potatoes, halved or quartered, depending on size*

1. Wash and dry lamb. Coat all over with flour. Heat margarine or dripping in pan. Add lamb and fry briskly until brown.
2. Mix in all remaining ingredients except potatoes. Bring to boil. Lower heat. Cover. Simmer for 1 hour or until meat is just tender, stirring occasionally.
3. Add potatoes. Cover pan again. Cook for a further 20 to 25 minutes or until potatoes are tender.

Serves 4

Chili Lamb

An economical dish from New Zealand. Serve with rice.

1 tablespoon salad oil
8 oz (225 g) onions, chopped
1 New Zealand lamb knuckle side of shoulder, cubed
1 to 2 level teaspoons mild chili powder
14 oz (400 g) can tomatoes
4 oz (125 g) button mushrooms, sliced
15 oz (425 g) can red kidney beans, drained and rinsed
1 to 1½ level teaspoons salt
½ level teaspoon Pizza seasoning herbs, oregano or basil

1. Heat oil in pan until sizzling. Add onions and lamb cubes. Fry until both are golden brown, allowing about 12 to 15 minutes.
2. Stir in chili powder, tomatoes, mushrooms, beans, salt and herbs. Pour in enough boiling water to cover the meat.
3. Bring to boil, stirring. Lower heat. Cover. Simmer gently for 1½ hours.

Serves 4

Moussaka

A Greek favourite based on lamb and aubergines which is rich, tasty and satisfying. My version uses poached aubergine slices instead of fried for a less oily result. A fresh-tasting mixed salad goes beautifully with this dish.

1 lb (450 g) aubergines
½ teaspoon lemon juice
1 level teaspoon salt
2 tablespoons salad oil
8 oz (225 g) onions, chopped
1 garlic clove, crushed
1 lb (450 g) boned leg of lamb, minced (use raw meat)
12 oz (350 g) tomatoes, blanched, skinned and chopped
3 level tablespoons tomato purée
1 level teaspoon dried marjoram or oregano
1 level tablespoon flour

Topping
1 oz (25 g) butter or margarine
1 oz (25 g) flour
½ pint (275 ml) milk
salt and pepper
1 Grade 3 egg
3 oz (75 g) Cheddar cheese, grated
salt and pepper

1. Wash and dry aubergines and remove green stems. Slice thinly. Put into frying pan. Add lemon juice, salt and enough water to cover. Bring to boil. Lower heat. Cover. Cook for 2 minutes. Drain.
2. Heat oil in pan. Add onions and garlic. Fry for about 10 minutes until light gold, turning frequently.
3. Add lamb. Increase heat slightly. Fry, fork-stirring all the time, until well browned and crumbly. Add tomatoes, purée, marjoram or oregano and flour. Cook for 5 minutes, stirring.
4. Cover base of 2½ pint (1½ litre) heatproof greased casserole with half the aubergine slices. Cover with an even layer of meat mixture. Finally add a layer of aubergines.

50

5. Make a white sauce. Melt butter or margarine in pan. Mix in flour and cook gently for 2 minutes, stirring. Gradually stir in milk. Cook until sauce comes to boil and thickens, stirring continually. Simmer for 2 minutes. Season.
6. Beat egg into sauce then stir in the cheese. Season to taste. Pour over casserole. Bake until well browned, allowing 45 minutes to 1 hour in moderately hot oven set to 190°C (375°F), Gas 5.

Serves 6 to 8

Moussaka with Potatoes
For a more economical version, follow recipe for Moussaka but use 1½ lb (675 g) boiled and sliced potatoes instead of aubergines.

Serves 6 to 8

Moussaka with Beef
Follow recipe for Moussaka but use minced beef instead of lamb.

Serves 4 to 6

Slimmers' Moussaka

I had better qualify this straight away by saying it is not a true moussaka but a layered meat and aubergine relation topped with cheese and eggs. No extra fat is added and there is no starchy thickener, so all in all this is a bonus for those who are watching their figures but still like to tuck into a flavoursome meal. Serve with a green vegetable which is low in calories.

1½ lb (675 g) aubergines, washed and dried
1 lb (450 g) very lean raw minced beef
1 14 oz (400 g) can tomatoes
1 level teaspoon basil
1 level teaspoon salt
1 garlic clove, crushed
4 oz (125 g) Cheddar cheese, grated
2 Grade 3 eggs

1. Wash aubergines and slice, removing green stalky ends. Drop into a large bowl of cold, salted water. Leave to soak for 30 minutes to remove bitter taste.
2. Lift out of bowl, squeeze dry in hands then cook in boiling salted water for 3 minutes. Drain.
3. Cover base of a 10-inch (25-cm) round and lightly oiled shallow casserole with half the aubergine slices. Top with meat, well mixed with tomatoes, basil, salt and garlic.
4. Cover meat with rest of aubergine slices then spread with the cheese, first beaten with eggs. Bake until bubbling and golden, allowing 45 minutes in a moderately hot oven set to 190°C (375°F), Gas 5.

Serves 6 to 8

Tex-Mex Lamb

A tasty, peppery adaptation of Chili Con Carne. It is easy to make and is quite delicious. Try serving it with a salad made of 1 large diced avocado and sliced tomatoes mixed with French dressing, and garnished with parsley or chives.

1 lb (900 g) New Zealand neck chops
3 level tablespoons flour
2 oz (50 g) margarine
4 oz (125 g) onions, chopped
4 oz (125 g) green pepper, cut into strips
14 oz (400 g) can tomatoes
1 to 2 level teaspoons chili powder
1 pint (575 ml) chicken stock
1 to 2 level teaspoons salt
4 oz (125 g) elbow or other short macaroni

1. Wash and dry chops. Toss in flour. Heat margarine in shallow pan. Add chops. Fry on both sides until well browned, turning once.
2. Remove to plate. Add onions and peppers to remaining margarine in pan. Fry gently until light gold.
3. Add tomatoes and juice from can. Squash against sides of pan to crush. Stir in chili powder, stock and salt.
4. Bring to boil and replace chops. Lower heat. Cover. Simmer gently for 1 hour, stirring occasionally.
5. Mix in macaroni. Continue to cook for a further 20 to 30 minutes or until tender, thinning down with a little extra boiling water if gravy seems too thick.

Serves 4

Lamb Cobbler

An oven-cooked casserole with an airy-light savoury scone topping. It makes an excellent main course and will be appreciated by all the family.

$1\frac{1}{2}$ oz (40 g) butter or margarine
8 oz (225 g) onions, chopped
4 oz (225 g) carrots, thinly sliced
4 oz (225 g) parsnip, cut into very small cubes
4 medium celery stalks, chopped
2 oz (50 g) pearl barley
2 lb (900 g) stewing lamb, divided into 8 pieces with surplus fat
   removed
1 oz (25 g) flour
2 level teaspoons salt
$\frac{1}{2}$ level teaspoon rosemary
$\frac{1}{2}$ pint (275 ml) hot water

Topping
8 oz (225 g) self-raising flour
1 level teaspoon baking powder
1 level teaspoon salt
1 level teaspoon mustard powder
2 oz (50 g) butter or margarine
8 tablespoons cold milk to mix
1 Grade 4 egg, beaten

1. Heat butter or margarine in pan. Add chopped vegetables. Fry for about 10 to 12 minutes until golden. Stir in barley. Arrange over the base of a large greased casserole, which should be wide rather than narrow and deep.
2. Coat lamb with flour. Arrange on top of vegetables. Sprinkle with salt and rosemary. Pour hot water into dish. Cover closely with lid or greased foil. Cook $1\frac{3}{4}$ hours in moderate oven set to 180°C (350°F), Gas 4.
3. To make topping, sift flour, baking powder, salt and mustard into bowl. Rub in butter or margarine. Using a fork, mix to soft dough

with milk. Turn on to floured surface. Knead dough lightly until smooth.
4. Cut into about 18 rounds with $1\frac{1}{2}$-inch (4-cm) cutter. Take casserole out of oven and uncover. Top with scones. Brush with egg. Return to hot oven set to 230°C (450°F), Gas 8. Bake for 15 minutes or until scones are well risen and golden.

Serves 4 to 6

Beef Cobbler
Follow recipe for Lamb Cobbler but use $1\frac{1}{2}$ lb (675 g) cubed braising steak instead of lamb. Cook for $2\frac{1}{4}$ hours in oven before topping with scones.

Peachy Lamb Special

Simmered in Portuguese rosé wine and enhanced by the addition of peaches, this is a special stew for those who enjoy something out of the ordinary.

2 oz (50 g) butter or margarine
2 large celery stalks, sliced
4 oz (125 g) red pepper, cut into strips
4 oz (125 g) onions, chopped
1½ lb (675 g) leg of lamb, cubed (boned weight)
3 level tablespoons flour
1 to 2 level teaspoons salt
15 oz (425 g) can peach slices
¾ pint (425 ml) rosé wine
4 oz (125 g) fresh bean sprouts
1 lb (450 g) potatoes, quartered

1. Heat margarine in pan. Add celery, pepper strips and onions. Fry gently, turning, for about 7 to 10 minutes until pale gold.
2. Increase heat. Add lamb. Fry fairly briskly until well sealed and browned.
3. Stir in flour and cook a further 2 minutes, turning. Add salt, peach slices and wine. Bring to boil. Lower heat. Cover.
4. Simmer gently for 1 hour. Add bean sprouts and potatoes. Mix in well. Cover. Continue to cook for a further 30 minutes.

Serves 4

Turkish Winter Stew

One always thinks of Turkey bathed in scorching sun, but its winters are bitingly cold and this stew, warming and hardy, is appropriate for chilly days.

2 tablespoons salad oil
8 oz (225 g) onions, finely chopped
1 garlic clove, sliced
8 oz (225 g) carrots, cut into 8 long strips
1 lb (450 g) boned leg of lamb, cubed
1 level tablespoon flour
½ pint (275 ml) water
6 oz (175 g) green pepper, cut into strips
2 level teaspoons salt
1 bouquet garni
1 medium lemon, sliced
1 lb (450 g) potatoes, halved or quartered, depending on size
15 oz (425 g) can butter beans, drained

1. Heat oil in heavy pan. Add onions, garlic and carrots. Fry over medium heat for about 15 minutes or until a warm gold. Remove from pan.
2. Wash and dry lamb. Add to pan, a few pieces at a time. Fry until well sealed and brown. Return vegetables to pan.
3. Work in flour. Gradually add water. Cook, stirring, until mixture comes to boil and thickens. Add pepper, salt, bouquet garni and lemon. Cover. Simmer for 1½ hours or until meat is just tender. Remove bouquet garni.
4. Add potatoes. Mix in well. Cook, covered, for a further 20 minutes. Stir in beans, cover again and continue to simmer for a further 5 to 7 minutes to heat beans.

Serves 4

Minted Lamb
and Butter Bean Stew

A whisper of flavours blended subtly together to create a lamb stew of style.

> *2 lb (900 g) stewing lamb, divided into large pieces with surplus fat removed*
> *2 level tablespoons flour*
> *1 oz (25 g) margarine or bacon dripping*
> *1 teaspoon salad oil*
> *8 oz (225 g) mange tout, topped and tailed*
> *8 oz (225 g) tomatoes, blanched, skinned and chopped*
> *$\frac{3}{4}$ pint (425 ml) chicken stock*
> *2 level tablespoons redcurrant jelly*
> *1 heaped tablespoon chopped fresh mint or 1 level teaspoon dried mint*
> *1 to 1$\frac{1}{2}$ level teaspoons salt*
> *15 oz (425 g) can butter beans, drained*
> *2 level teaspooons paprika*

1. Wash and dry lamb pieces then coat with flour. Heat margarine or dripping and the oil in pan. Add lamb and fry until well browned. Tip any leftover flour into pan and fry for a further 1 minute.
2. Mix in mange tout, tomatoes, stock, redcurrant jelly, mint and salt. Bring to boil, stirring. Lower heat. Cover.
3. Simmer gently for 1$\frac{1}{2}$ to 1$\frac{3}{4}$ hours or until lamb is tender, stirring occasionally.
4. Top with a layer of beans, sprinkle with paprika and replace lid. Cook for a further 15 minutes.

Serves 4

Lamb and Gammon Casserole

A main course of many meats embraced with mixed vegetables and apple juice.

12 oz (350 g) stewing lamb, boned and cut into small pieces
6 oz (175 g) lamb's liver, cubed
2 level tablespoons flour
2 oz (50 g) margarine
8 oz (225 g) onions, chopped
4 oz (125 g) gammon, chopped
8 oz (225 g) cooking apples, peeled, cored and thinly sliced
2 oz (50 g) turnip, cut into small dice
4 oz (125 g) swede, cut into small dice
8 oz (225 g) broad beans
1 pint (575 ml) apple juice
2 level teaspoons salt
1 level teaspoon prepared English mustard
1 level teaspoon mixed herbs
1 lb (450 g) potatoes, halved or quartered, depending on size

1. Wash and dry lamb and liver then coat all over with flour.
2. Heat margarine in large pan. Add onions and gammon. Fry over medium heat until pale gold. Mix in lamb and liver. Increase heat. Fry fairly briskly until well sealed and brown.
3. Stir in apples, turnip, swede, beans, apple juice, salt, mustard and herbs. Bring to boil, stirring.
4. Lower heat. Cover. Simmer for $1\frac{1}{4}$ hours, stirring occasionally. Add potatoes and continue to cook, covered, for a further 25 to 30 minutes or until tender.

Serves 4 to 6

Bobotie with Lamb

A South African speciality, well worth trying by those who enjoy hearty food interestingly presented. Serve with freshly boiled rice and chutney.

> *3 oz (75 g) flaked almonds*
> *2 large slices white bread, cubed*
> *½ pint (275 ml) warm milk*
> *1 garlic clove, crushed*
> *3 oz (75 g) onions, grated*
> *2 lb (900 g) raw leg of lamb, diced and minced*
> *2 level teaspoons salt*
> *pepper*
> *1 to 2 level tablespoons hot or mild curry powder*
> *4 Grade 3 eggs*
> *salt*

1. Tip almonds into bowl. Add bread, half the milk, garlic, onions, lamb, salt, pepper, curry powder and 2 eggs. Mix very thoroughly.
2. Spread evenly into greased casserole dish. Cover with lid or buttered foil and bake for 45 minutes in moderate oven set to 180°C (350°F), Gas 4.
3. Uncover Bobotie and coat with rest of milk, beaten with remaining 2 eggs. Return to oven. Bake for 30 to 40 minutes until top is golden brown.

Serves 6

Bobotie with Beef
Make exactly as the above recipe but use minced raw beef instead of lamb.

Lamb Hotpot

Appetisingly enriched with Scotch Broth soup, this is a Lancashire style hotpot with a fine flavour. (See illustration facing page 65.)

2 lb (900 g) potatoes
2 lb (900 g) best end neck of lamb
4 lambs' kidneys
12 oz (350 g) onions
1½ cans condensed Scotch Broth soup
1½ oz (40 g) butter or margarine, melted

1. Slice potatoes thinly. Trim away surplus fat from lamb and discard. Skin kidneys and halve. Remove centre cores and cut flesh into small pieces.
2. Place just over half the potatoes in a large greased casserole. Spread with lamb and kidneys. Cover with undiluted soup.
3. Arrange rest of potatoes on top. Brush with melted butter or margarine. Cover. Cook 1¾ hours in moderate oven set to 180°C (350°F), Gas 4. Uncover. Continue to cook for a further 30 to 45 minutes to brown and glaze potatoes and fully tenderise the meat.

Serves 6

Scottish Style Beef Hotpot

Make as above recipe but use 1½ lb (675 g) cubed braising steak instead of lamb. Cook for 2 hours before uncovering and browning the top.

Lamb and Apple Tasty

Fragrant with apples and onion, here is a splendid layered casserole for winter eating.

3 oz (75 g) butter or margarine
4 New Zealand lamb shoulder cuts
6 oz (175 g) onions, chopped
12 oz (350 g) cooking apples, peeled, cored and chopped
2 lb (900 g) potatoes, very thinly sliced
1 level teaspoon soft brown sugar
salt and pepper
½ pint (275 ml) chicken stock

1. Heat 2 oz (50 g) butter or margarine in pan. Add lamb slices. Fry on both sides until well sealed and golden. Remove to plate.
2. Add onions and apples to pan. Fry over medium heat for 5 minutes. Draw pan aside. Cover base of greased casserole with half the potato slices.
3. Arrange shoulder cuts, in single layer, on top then coat with fried onion and apples. Season with sugar, salt and pepper to taste. Cover with a layer of remaining potatoes. Pour over stock.
4. Melt remaining 1 oz (25 g) butter or margarine and trickle over potatoes. Bake, uncovered, for 1 hour in moderate oven set to 180°C (350°F), Gas 4.

Serves 4

Lamb and Apple Shandy
Make as previous recipe but omit sugar and use canned shandy instead of stock.

Lamb with Haricots

Pleasingly economical, here is a recipe from the country where they know more about lamb than anywhere else—New Zealand. Serve it with creamed potatoes.

4 oz (125 g) haricot beans, soaked overnight
1 pint (575 ml) water
1 tablespoon salad oil
4 New Zealand lamb leg shanks
14 oz (400 g) can tomatoes
8 oz (225 g) onions, sliced
4 medium celery stalks, sliced
2 level teaspons salt
1 heaped tablespoon chopped parsley

1. Drain beans and put into pan with water. Bring to boil. Cover. Simmer for 30 minutes.
2. Meanwhile, heat oil in separate pan and fry lamb shanks until well browned. Add to pan of beans with all remaining ingredients.
3. Bring to boil. Skim. Lower heat. Cover. Simmer for about 1 to $1\frac{1}{2}$ hours or until beans are completely tender. Stir occasionally.

Serves 4

Lamb and Ladyfinger Curry

A hint of the Orient characterises this mild and subtle curry.

2 oz (50 g) butter or ghee
2 teaspoons salad oil
8 oz (225 g) onions, chopped
2 garlic cloves, sliced
1½ lb (675 g) boned leg of lamb, cut into small cubes
3 rounded teaspoons medium hot curry powder
3 rounded teaspoons garam masala (seasoning mix for curry, available from supermarkets and Asian food shops)
3 rounded teaspoons tomato purée
1 to 1½ level teaspoons salt
3 heaped tablespoons natural yogurt
½ pint (275 ml) water
1 rounded tablespoon mango chutney
1 tablespoon lemon juice
1 lb (450 g) potatoes, cut into chunks
1¾ lb (792 g) can okra (ladies' fingers), drained but unrinsed

1. Heat butter or ghee and oil in heavy-based pan. Add onions and garlic. Fry, covered, over medium heat until soft. Uncover. Continue to fry fairly briskly until pale gold.
2. Add lamb, a few cubes at a time. Fry until well-sealed and brown. Stir in all the ingredients except the potatoes and okra.
3. Bring to boil and cover. Lower heat. Simmer for 1½ hours. Add potatoes. Cover again. Simmer for a further 20 minutes. Gently stir in okra. Heat through, covered, for 10 minutes.

Serves 6

Right: Lamb Braise with Cabbage (page 42).

Pilau of Lamb

Also called pilaff or pilav, this is the oriental answer to Italy's risotto and makes a marvellous all-in-one main course, suitable all the year round.

3 tablespoons salad oil
1 lb (450 g) neck of lamb fillet, cut into narrow strips
8 oz (225 g) onions, chopped
1 to 2 oz (25 to 50 g) pine nuts
1 lb (450 g) easy-cook round grain rice
2 oz (50 g) currants
2 medium tomatoes, blanched, skinned and chopped
½ level teaspoon cinnamon
2 pints (1¼ litres) chicken stock
salt and pepper

1. Heat oil in pan. Add lamb and onions. Fry gently until deep gold. Stir in nuts and rice. Continue to fry until they just begin to turn golden.
2. Add currants, tomatoes, cinnamon and stock. Season to taste with salt and pepper. Bring to boil. Lower heat and cover. Simmer for 15 minutes. Remove from heat.
3. Uncover. Place a clean, folded teatowel on top of rice then cover with saucepan lid. Leave to stand for 20 minutes before serving, or until rice is completely dry.

Serves 8

Pilau of Turkey

Make as pilau of Lamb but use 1 lb (450 g) turkey breast fillet instead of lamb.

Left: Lamb Hotpot (page 61).

Lemony Lamb Stew

Strewn with crackling sesame seeds and served sizzling hot, here is a succulent lamb dish with a subtle tang of lemon.

3 lb (1½ kg) neck of lamb, divided into neat portions and with surplus fat removed
½ pint (275 ml) dry vintage cider
1 level teaspoon brown sugar
8 oz (225 g) onions, chopped
12 oz (350 g) tomatoes, blanched, skinned and chopped
1 large lemon, thinly sliced
2 beef stock cubes
1 level teaspoon salt
8 oz (225 g) button mushrooms
1 lb (450 g) potatoes, quartered if large or left whole if small
2 level tablespoons cornflour
4 tablespoons cold water
1 heaped tablespoon sesame seeds, toasted under grill until lightly brown

1. Wash and dry lamb. Put into large pan. Add cider, sugar, onions, tomatoes and lemon slices. Crumble in stock cubes. Add salt.
2. Bring to boil, stirring. Lower heat. Cover. Simmer gently for 1½ hours. Add mushrooms and potatoes. Continue to cook for a further 15 minutes or until the potatoes are tender.
3. To thicken, mix cornflour with water until smooth. Add to lamb, stirring until it bubbles. Simmer for a further 10 minutes. Transfer to a warm serving dish and sprinkle with sesame seeds.

Serves 4

Pork and Bacon

Pork in the Normandy Style

A lovely savoury pork dish with a slightly sweet-sour flavour.

1 lb (450 g) boiled potatoes
3 oz (75 g) butter or margarine, melted
4 oz (125 g) onions, sliced
4 pork chops, each about 6 oz (175 g)
1 oz (25 g) flour
¼ pint (150 ml) medium sweet cider
¼ pint (150 ml) chicken stock
½ level teaspoon sage
salt and pepper
1 medium cooking apple, peeled and cored
watercress for garnish

1. Grate potatoes coarsely and mix with half the melted butter or margarine. Use to line a well-greased casserole that is wide and shallow rather than narrow and deep.
2. Pour rest of butter or margarine into pan. Add onions. Fry until pale gold. Lift out with draining spoon and sprinkle over the potatoes.
3. Add chops to pan and fry briskly until well browned on both sides, turning once. Arrange, in single layer, on top of potato mixture.
4. Stir flour into rest of butter or margarine in pan and cook for 1 minute. Gradually blend in cider and stock. Cook, stirring, until mixture comes to boil and thickens. Season to taste with sage, salt and pepper.
5. Pour sauce over chops and potato mixture in dish. Cut apple into 4 thick slices. Place 1 slice on each chop. Bake, uncovered, for 40 minutes in moderate oven set to 180°C (350°F), Gas 4. Garnish with watercress.

Serves 4

Veal Chops Normandy
Make as above but use 4 veal chops instead of pork.

68

Pork Layer Casserole

A spectacular pork dish which looks as good as it tastes, and can be quickly made from the remains of the Sunday roast. (See illustration facing page 96.)

1 oz (25 g) butter
6 oz (175 g) onions, chopped
1 lb (450 g) cold roast pork, cut into cubes
¼ pint (125 ml) leftover gravy, boiling
1 tablespoon mushroom ketchup
1 small cabbage
8 oz (125 g) American long grain rice
1 pint (475 ml) beef stock
2 medium carrots, thinly sliced
1 small turnip, thinly sliced

1. Melt butter in casserole and fry onion gently for 10 minutes. Add pork, gravy and mushroom ketchup. Cook gently for 5 minutes.
2. Place layer of cabbage leaves over meat, then add a layer of rice. Cover with layer of carrots and turnips.
3. Pour stock gently over the top. Cover. Simmer for 20 to 25 minutes until rice is tender, or bake in oven set to 200° C (400° F), Gas 6 for 35 minutes.

Serves 4

Creole Pork

A winner of an easy dish, and delicious into the bargain!

4 pork chops, each about 6 oz (175 g)
1 rounded tablespoon flour
2 oz (50 g) butter, margarine or lard
4 oz (125 g) onions, grated
3 oz (75 g) green pepper, finely chopped
4 oz (125 g) button mushrooms, sliced
12 oz (350 g) potatoes, grated
1 can condensed tomato soup
1 level teaspoon finely grated orange peel
3 tablespoons boiling water
1 to 1½ level teaspoons salt
1 heaped tablespoon finely chopped parsley

1. Wash and dry chops then coat generously with flour. Fry in hot fat until brown and crisp on both sides, turning once. Remove to plate for time being.
2. Add onions and green pepper to remaining fat in pan. Fry for about 7 to 10 minutes or until golden brown. Transfer to greased casserole. Sprinkle with mushrooms and potatoes.
3. Arrange chops, in single layer, on top. Mix the remaining ingredients together except parsley. Spoon over chops.
4. Cover with lid or greased foil. Bake for 1¼ to 1½ hours in centre of moderate oven set to 180°C (350°F), Gas 4. Uncover and sprinkle with parsley before serving.

Serves 4

Creole Liver

Make exactly as above but use 1 lb (450 g) sliced ox liver, first soaked for 30 minutes in cold milk as this removes the strong taste. Dry thoroughly before coating with flour.

Pork and Asparagus Layer

A surprise package of a pork dish with a very special luxurious flavour to tempt family and friends.

2 oz (50 g) butter or margarine
2 teaspoons salad oil
8 oz (225 g) onions, chopped
4 pork chops each about 6 oz (175 g), trimmed of surplus fat
1½ lb (675 g) potatoes, grated
1 can condensed cream of asparagus soup
3 tablespoons medium sherry
½ to 1 level teaspoon salt
white pepper

1. Heat 1 oz (25 g) margarine and the oil in a large frying pan. Add onions and fry until pale gold. Move to one side of pan.
2. Wash and dry chops. Add to pan, two at a time, and fry on both sides until crisp and well browned.
3. Cover base of greased, oblong heatproof dish with half the potatoes. Top with a single layer of fried onions and chops.
4. Tip soup and sherry into pan. Heat gently, whisking all the time, until smooth. Season to taste with salt and pepper and pour over chops.
5. Top with an even layer of remaining potatoes. Melt rest of butter or margarine. Trickle over potatoes. Cook, uncovered, for 45 minutes in moderately hot oven set to 200°C (400°F), Gas 6.

Serves 4

Farmer's Pork and Potato Pie

A budget-minded pie based on minced pork belly and beef sausagemeat, topped with a snow-like mass of fluffy potatoes and grated cheese.

1 lb (450 g) pork belly
4 oz (125 g) onions
8 oz (225 g) beef sausages
1 garlic clove, crushed
2 Grade 3 eggs, beaten
$\frac{1}{4}$ pint (150 ml) milk
$\frac{1}{2}$ level teaspoon dried sage
1 level teaspoon paprika
1 to $1\frac{1}{2}$ level teaspoons salt
1 small packet instant mashed potatoes (2 to 3 servings)
3 oz (75 g) Cheddar cheese, grated

1. Remove rind and bones from pork belly and cut flesh into cubes. Peel onions and cut into chunks. Mince both finely together.
2. Skin sausages (unless you buy skinned ones or sausagemeat). Stir into pork mixture. Add garlic.
3. Fork in eggs, milk, sage, paprika and salt. Mix thoroughly. Spread evenly into greased heatproof casserole.
4. Bake, covered, for $1\frac{1}{4}$ hours in moderately hot oven set to 190°C (375°F),Gas 5. Uncover. Cook for a further 15 minutes.
5. Remove from oven, top with potatoes made up as directed on the packet, then sprinkle with cheese. Brown quickly under a hot grill.

Serves 6 to 8

72

Westphalian Bean Soup

North European soups tend to be the equivalent of our own casseroles or hotpots and this hearty brew is no exception. Served with thick slices of wholemeal or rye bread and butter, it is a complete meal in a plate—with the added advantage of being reasonably economical to make.

8 oz (225 g) haricot beans
2½ pints (1½ litres) water
1½ lb (675 g) unsalted belly of pork, in one piece
4 oz (125 g) carrots, sliced
8 oz (225 g) onions, thinly sliced
8 oz (225 g) leek, trimmed with 3 inches (7½ cm) green 'skirt' left and
*   sliced*
4 oz (125 g) swede, diced
2 large celery stalks, sliced
1 level tablespoon salt
4 oz (125 g) green beans (whole)
2 heaped tablespoons chopped parsley

1. Wash beans and soak overnight in the water. Tip both beans and water into large pan. Bring to boil. Lower heat. Skim. Cover. Simmer for 1½ hours.
2. Add all remaining ingredients except green beans and parsley. Bring to boil again. Cover. Simmer for a further 1½ hours or until haricot beans are very soft.
3. Remove pork belly and cube flesh. Dice skin and fry until crisp in a little oil. Return both to pan with green beans and parsley.
4. Heat through for a further 10 minutes, season to taste and serve very hot in deep plates.

Serves 6

Boston Baked Beans

Adapted from an authentic recipe passed on to me in Boston itself—home of this famous dish. Serve with wholemeal bread.

1 lb (450 g) haricot beans, soaked overnight in water
1 pint (575 ml) water
1 lb (450 g) salted belly of pork, well washed and cubed
1 level tablespoon mustard powder
3 oz (75 g) dark brown soft sugar
3 level tablespoons black treacle or mollasses, if available
3 level tablespoons tomato purée
3 cloves
1 large onion

1. Drain beans. Tip into saucepan. Add water. Bring to boil. Skim. Lower heat. Cover. Simmer for $1\frac{1}{2}$ hours. Strain, reserving liquid.
2. Place pork in large casserole then sprinkle with beans. Mix reserved liquid with mustard, sugar, treacle or mollasses and purée. Pour into casserole, making sure it covers beans. If not, add extra water.
3. Press cloves into whole onion then 'bury' in the beans. Cover closely with lid or greased foil. Cook very slowly for 8 hours in cool oven set to 150°C (300°F), Gas 2. At this stage beans should be tender but, if not, return to oven for a further 30 to 45 minutes.
4. Check every 2 hours or so to see that liquid level is being maintained and top up with boiling water if necessary. Serve very hot.

Serves 6

Pork and Beans in Cider

Flavoured with cider and laced with apples and raisins, here is a tempting pork dish which needs very little by way of extras and is ideal for an informal gathering of friends. Serve with jacket potatoes baked at the same time as the pork.

2 oz (50 g) butter or margarine
1 lb (450 g) lean stewing pork, diced
1 lb (450 g) swede, coarsely chopped
2 large leeks, sliced
1 large cooking apple, peeled, cored and thinly sliced
2 oz (50 g) seedless raisins
½ pint (275 ml) dry cider
15 oz (425 g) can baked beans in tomato sauce
1 level teaspoon salt

1. Heat butter or margarine in pan. Add pork. Fry fairly briskly until well browned and sealed. Place in large greased casserole.
2. Add vegetables and apples to remaining butter or margarine in pan. Fry until pale gold, allowing about 10 minutes and turning fairly frequently. Add to casserole with all remaining ingredients. Mix thoroughly.
3. Cover closely with lid or greased foil. Cook for 1½ hours in moderate oven set to 180°C (350°F), Gas 4.

Serves 4

Pork Curry

Choose a lean cut of pork—such as chump end of loin—and you have a winner of a pork curry with a robust flavour and a lovely colour. Serve with freshly cooked rice, fruit chutney and a mixture of four heaped tablespoons natural yogurt flavoured with half a level teaspoon chopped fresh mint.

1 portion curried sauce 'Wagar' (page 162), defrosted
2 tablespoons lemon juice
1 rounded tablespoon mango chutney
1 lb (450 g) chump end pork loin, cubed
1 level teaspoon salt

1. Spoon sauce into pan. Stir in lemon juice and chutney. Bring to boil, stirring.
2. Add pork cubes and salt. Mix in well. Cover. Simmer for $1\frac{1}{4}$ to $1\frac{1}{2}$ hours, stirring from time to time to prevent sticking.

Serves 4

Yugoslav Stew

A typically Balkan juicy meat stew made with two different meats.

1 lb (450 g) pork fillet
1 lb (450 g) sirloin steak
1 lb (450 g) onions, sliced in rings
1 lb (450 g) aubergines, unpeeled and diced
1 lb red and/or green peppers, cut into strips
6 tablespoons salad oil
8 oz (225 g) easy-cook long grain rice
1¾ pints (1 litre) chicken stock
1 level teaspoon marjoram
2 × 14 oz (400 g) cans tomatoes
3 to 4 level teaspoons salt

1. Cut both meats into thin strips.
2. Heat oil in heavy-based pan. Add meat and all the prepared vegetables. Fry over fairly brisk heat for about 20 to 25 minutes or until golden brown, stirring from time to time.
3. Mix in rice. Fry for 2 minutes. Add stock, marjoram, tomatoes and salt. Bring to boil, stirring. Lower heat. Cover. Simmer for 35 to 40 minutes, stirring a few times with a fork. Serve very hot.

Serves 6 to 8

Chinese Pork and Pepper Pot

An easy-to-make dish, designed for lovers of Chinese food. Serve with freshly cooked bean sprouts tossed with a dash of sesame oil and two teaspoons soy sauce.

2 tablespoons salad oil
1 garlic clove, crushed
2 lb (900 g) stewing pork, cut into short strips
$\frac{3}{4}$ pint (425 ml) water
2 tablespoons dry sherry
2 tablespoons soy sauce
8 oz (225 g) green peppers, cut into strips
2 level teaspoons dark brown soft sugar
1 tablespoon malt vinegar
6 oz (175 g) button mushrooms, sliced
6 oz (175 g) vermicelli

1. Heat oil in pan. Add garlic and pork. Fry until lightly browned, stirring. Mix in water, sherry and soy sauce.
2. Bring to boil. Lower heat. Cover. Simmer for 1 to $1\frac{1}{2}$ hours or until pork is tender. Add peppers, sugar and vinegar. Continue to cook for 15 minutes. Mix in mushrooms and vermicelli. Cover. Cook for 10 to 12 minutes or until vermicelli is tender.

Serves 6

Chinese Duck and Pepper Pot
Enlist the help of a cooperative butcher. Ask him to chop up a 3 lb ($1\frac{1}{2}$ kg) oven-ready duck into small pieces (including bones) then make exactly as Chinese Pork and Pepper Pot, but *do not* add mushrooms. Cover. Leave in a cool place overnight then remove layer of fat from the top. Before serving, reheat the mixture until hot then add mushrooms and noodles. Bring to the boil and cover. Boil gently for about 20 minutes or until vermicelli is tender.

Barbecued Beans and Bangers

Devotees of beans and sausages will love this recipe, which takes just a few minutes to put together. Serve with creamed or jacket potatoes.

2 oz (50 g) onion, chopped
2 tablespoons brown ketchup
2 tablespoons Worcestershire sauce
2 × 15 oz (425 g) cans baked beans in tomato sauce
1 lb (450 g) pork sausages

1. Mix first 4 ingredients well together. Tip into large casserole. Add sausages.
2. Cover securely with lid or greased foil. Cook for 45 minutes to 1 hour in moderate oven set to 180°C (350°F), Gas 4.

Serves 6

Cassoulet of Frankfurters

Based on a traditional French dish, this sausage 'brew' is wonderful for cold weather eating and will never leave you hungry! Eat it with pieces of crusty French bread.

2 level tablespoons flour
4 tablespoons water
1 lb (450 g) Frankfurter sausages
12 oz (350 g) unsalted belly of pork, rind removed
14 oz (400 g) can tomatoes
15 oz (425 g) can cannellini beans, drained
15 oz (425 g) can red kidney beans, drained
1 garlic clove, crushed (optional)
8 oz (225 g) onions, sliced
4 medium celery stalks, sliced
1 tablespoon Worcestershire sauce
1 rounded tablespoon Muscavado sugar
1 pint (575 ml) beef stock

1. Mix flour to smooth paste with cold water. Halve sausages. Cut pork into bite-sized pieces.
2. Put the flour paste, sausages and pork into large casserole. Add tomatoes, both types of beans, garlic, onions, celery, Worcestershire sauce, sugar and stock. Mix thoroughly. Cover securely with lid or greased foil. Cook for 2 hours in cool oven set to 160°C (325°F), Gas 3.

Serves 6

Cumberland Sausage Casserole

A surprise package, using a British speciality. Cumberland sausage ring, with its mild flavour and pale colour, makes a treat of a meal when served with small boiled potatoes in their skins, and orange slices warmed through in a little honey and sprinkled with cloves. (See illustration facing page 112.)

1 lb (450 g) Cumberland sausage ring
1 lb (450 g) red cabbage, finely shredded
6 oz (175 g) onions, peeled and chopped
2 red-skinned dessert apples, unpeeled then quartered, cored and
   sliced
2 rounded teaspoons juniper berries
½ pint (275 ml) dry cider
3 level tablespoons redcurrant jelly
1½ tablespoons malt vinegar
salt and pepper

1. Put sausage into large casserole with cabbage, onions, apples and juniper berries.
2. Heat cider with redcurrant jelly and vinegar until jelly melts. Season to taste with salt and pepper.
3. Pour into casserole. Cover closely and cook for 2½ to 3 hours in cool oven set to 150°C (300°F), Gas 2.

Serves 6

Sausage Goulash

An unusual but delicious goulash which is very quickly made.

1½ oz (40 g) butter, margarine or dripping
1 lb (450 g) pork sausages
4 oz (125 g) green pepper, chopped
4 oz (125 g) onions, chopped
2 level teaspoons paprika
10 oz (275 g) courgettes, sliced
salt and pepper
5 oz (142 ml) carton soured cream

1. Heat butter, margarine or dripping in pan. Add sausages and fry for 10 to 12 minutes or until well browned.
2. Cut sausages into chunks and set aside. Add green pepper and onions to remaining fat in pan. Fry gently until golden, allowing about 7 to 10 minutes.
3. Stir in paprika. Replace sausages then mix in courgettes. Season to taste with salt and pepper. Cover. Simmer over very low heat for 15 to 20 minutes or until courgettes are soft.
4. Mix in soured cream and heat through for a further 5 minutes, stirring. Serve very hot.

Serves 4

Sausage Paprika

An authentically-flavoured Hungarian-style paprika dish which is surprisingly good made with a combination of sausages and salami. (See illustration facing page 97.)

3 tablespoons salad oil
8 oz (225 g) onions, chopped
2 garlic cloves, crushed
4 oz (125 g) green pepper, chopped
4 oz (125 g) red pepper, chopped
1 rounded tablespoon paprika
½ level teaspoon salt
½ level teaspoon dried dill
14 oz (400 g) can tomatoes
1 lb (450 g) potatoes, cubed or sliced
1 lb (450 g) pork sausages, fried and sliced
4 oz (125 g) Hungarian salami, cut into strips
5 oz (142 ml) carton soured cream

1. Heat oil until hot in large pan. Add onions, garlic and both peppers and fry gently until golden, allowing about 12 to 15 minutes.
2. Stir in paprika, salt, dill, tomatoes and potatoes. Bring to boil. Cover. Simmer very gently for about 20 minutes. Add sausages, salami and soured cream. Warm through for a further 7 minutes, stirring.

Serves 4

Bacon and Vegetable Casserole

This is an excellent way of presenting forehock and makes a super summer casserole for evening eating. Serve with new potatoes, if liked. (See illustration facing page 113.)

> 2 lb (900 g) forehock of British bacon
> 2 level tablespoons flour
> 2 tablespoons salad oil
> 4 oz (125 g) onions, sliced
> 3 oz (75 g) carrots, cut into small dice
> 8 oz (225 g) courgettes, cut into small dice
> $\frac{1}{2}$ level teaspoon mixed herbs
> $\frac{1}{4}$ pint (125 ml) chicken stock
> $\frac{1}{4}$ pint (125 ml) dry red wine
> 1 rounded teaspoon clear honey
> black pepper

1. Put bacon into large pan. Cover with cold water and bring slowly to boil. Drain. Repeat twice more as this helps to reduce saltiness more effectively than soaking overnight.
2. Leave until cold. Cut into cubes, discarding fat and skin. Coat with flour.
3. Heat oil in pan. Add vegetables. Fry over medium heat until golden. Move to one side. Add bacon and any leftover flour. Fry a little more briskly until well sealed and crispy brown.
4. Add herbs, stock, wine, honey and pepper. Mix well. Bring to boil, stirring. Lower heat. Cover. Simmer gently for 2 hours, stirring occasionally.

Serves 6

Green Cabbage
and Bacon Casserole

Down-to-earth fare but wholesome and filling.

1½ lb (675 g) head of firm green cabbage
12 oz (350 g) gammon steaks, cubed
1 oz (25 g) butter or margarine
1 oz (25 g) flour
¾ pint (425 ml) tomato juice
2 level teaspoons soft brown sugar
1 lb (450 g) potatoes, coarsely grated
8 oz (225 g) tomatoes, blanched, skinned and chopped
2 medium celery stalks, sliced
salt and pepper

1. Discard any bruised and damaged outer leaves from cabbage then cut head into 12 wedges—rather like slices of cake. Cut out hard core.
2. Arrange, in single layer, over base of medium-sized deep greased casserole. Fry cubed gammon in butter or margarine until lightly browned.
3. Stir in flour then gradually blend in tomato juice. Cook, stirring, until mixture comes to boil and thickens. Add sugar then spoon over cabbage.
4. Surround with potatoes, tomatoes and celery. Season to taste with salt and pepper. Cover closely with lid or greased foil. Cook for 1½ hours in moderate oven set to 180°C (350°F), Gas 4.

Serves 4 to 6

Bacon and Barley Cheese

An unusual and particularly warming main course for winter which will win the approval of all those who, like me, love barley and feel it is very underrated. Serve with freshly cooked cabbage or sprouts.

6 oz (175 g) pearl barley
12 oz (350 g) back bacon, cut into strips
8 oz (225 g) onions, fairly coarsely chopped
1 pint (575 ml) water
½ to 1 level teaspoon salt, depending on saltiness of bacon
1 heaped tablespoon chopped parsley
1 level teaspoon prepared mustard
6 oz (175 g) Cheddar cheese, finely grated

1. Put barley into pan. Add bacon, onions, water and salt. Bring to boil, stirring. Lower heat. Cover.
2. Simmer gently for about 45 minutes to 1 hour or until barley is tender, topping up with boiling water every now and then if liquid seems to be evaporating too quickly.
3. Remove from heat. Stir in parsley, mustard and 4 oz (125 g) of the cheese. Spoon into greased casserole. Sprinkle top with remaining cheese and brown under a hot grill.

Serves 4

Sauerkraut and Bacon Braise

A robust, Central European, 'peasant' dish that is particularly filling.

2 oz (50 g) dripping
6 oz (175 g) onions, chopped
8 oz (225 g) cooking apples, peeled, cored and sliced
1 lb (450 g) canned or bottled sauerkraut
1½ level teaspoons salt
1 pint (575 ml) water
½ level teaspoon caraway seeds (optional)
2 level teaspoons castor sugar
2 lb (900 g) Danish bacon joint, such as prime fore-end
1½ lb (675 g) potatoes, halved or quartered, depending on size

1. Heat dripping in pan until sizzling. Add onions and apples. Cover. Fry over minimal heat for 20 minutes or until soft but not browned. Keep pan half covered with lid.
2. Stir in sauerkraut then add salt, water, caraway seeds (if used) and sugar. Bring slowly to boil, stirring. Cover.
3. Lower heat and simmer for 45 minutes stirring occasionally. Stand bacon joint on top. Continue to cook, covered, for a further 1 hour. Add potatoes, cover pan again and cook for another 20 minutes or until tender.
4. To serve, take joint out of pan and carve into slices. Transfer to warm plate and surround with sauerkraut mixture and potatoes.

Serves 6 to 8

Creamy Bacon
and Vegetable Bake

A quick and easy dish which uses up cold cooked potatoes.

1 can condensed cream of chicken soup
1 level teaspoon mustard powder
1 teaspoon Worcestershire sauce
1 lb (450 g) cold cooked potatoes, cut into cubes
8 oz (225 g) fresh runner beans or frozen French beans, thawed
6 oz (175 g) canned or frozen (thawed) sweetcorn
4 oz (125 g) Cheddar cheese, grated
4 rashers collar bacon
1 oz (25 g) butter or margarine

1. Mix soup with mustard and Worcestershire sauce. Add potatoes, beans, sweetcorn and cheese. Stir well.
2. Pour into greased casserole that is wide and shallow rather than deep. Arrange bacon rashers on top in a single layer.
3. Dot with flakes of butter or margarine. Cook, uncovered, for 30 to 35 minutes in moderately hot oven set to 200°C (400°F), Gas 6.

Serves 4

Savoury
Bread and Butter Pudding

A change from the sweet version and with an appetising flavour and tempting, golden crust.

3 large slices white bread
3 large slices brown bread
butter or margarine
4 oz (125 g) Cheddar cheese, grated
1 oz (25 g) mushrooms, thinly sliced
4 oz (125 g) lean ham, chopped
2 Grade 3 eggs
1 pint (575 ml) warm milk
1 level teaspoon continental mustard
1 teaspoon Worcestershire sauce
salt and pepper

1. Spread both kinds of bread thickly with butter or margarine then cut each slice into 4 squares.
2. Arrange half the squares, buttered sides up, over base of well-greased oblong or square heatproof dish which is shallow rather than deep.
3. Sprinkle with half the cheese, all the mushrooms and chopped ham. Top with rest of bread squares, buttered sides down.
4. Beat eggs with rest of ingredients then slowly pour into dish over bread mixture. Leave to stand for 20 minutes.
5. Bake until golden brown and puffy, allowing about 45 minutes in moderately hot oven set to 190°C (375°F), Gas 5.

Serves 4

Macaroni Carbonara

I can't think of an easier dish nor one with more chic than this Italian speciality. Serve with a side salad of tomatoes sprinkled with chopped onions and fresh parsley.

> 12 oz (350 g) penne *or other large pieces of macaroni*
> *2 teaspoons salad oil*
> *4 oz (125 g) mushrooms, thinly sliced*
> *2 oz (50 g) butter*
> *4 oz (125 g) best quality ham (use Parma if you like its distinctive flavour), cut into thin strips*
> *2 oz (50 g) Italian salami, cut into thin strips*
> *2 oz (50 g) small black olives*
> $\frac{1}{4}$ *pint (150 ml) single cream*
> *3 Grade 3 eggs*
> *3 oz (75 g) grated Parmesan cheese*

1. Cook macaroni in fast boiling salted water and oil (which stops it sticking) for about 12 minutes or until just tender. Do not over-cook, or macaroni will become slushy.
2. Meanwhile, fry mushrooms in the butter for 5 minutes.
3. Tip macaroni into colander to drain then return to pan in which it was cooked. Stand over low heat. Add mushrooms and butter in which they were fried, together with the ham, salami and olives.
4. Beat cream with eggs until very well blended. Tip into pan of macaroni with half the cheese.
5. Toss with two spoons until eggs are lightly scrambled and cling to the macaroni. Spoon out on to warm plates and sprinkle rest of cheese on top.

Serves 4

Macaroni Matriciana

This is a close relation of Macaroni Carbonara and is just as good!

8 oz (225 g) pieces of large sized macaroni
¼ pint (150 ml) single cream
2 Grade 3 eggs, well beaten
3 oz (75 g) Parma ham, chopped
8 oz (225 g) tomatoes, blanched, skinned and chopped
1 heaped tablespoon finely chopped parsley
salt and pepper
3 to 4 rounded tablespoons grated Parmesan cheese

1. Cook macaroni in fast boiling salted water for about 15 minutes or until just tender. Drain and return to pan.
2. Stand over low heat. Add cream, eggs, ham, tomatoes and parsley. Season to taste then, using two spoons, toss mixture thoroughly.
3. When ready, the eggs should be lightly scrambled and the mixture piping hot. Transfer to four plates and sprinkle with the Parmesan cheese.

Serves 4

Country Cottage Hotpot

Packed with freshness and well-endowed with all the good things of life, this is a quick-to-bake hotpot which is both lively and appetising.

2 large leeks
2 lb (900 g) potatoes, quartered
1½ oz (40 g) butter or margarine
4 oz (125 g) gammon, chopped
1½ oz (40 g) flour
¾ pint (425 ml) cold milk
8 oz (225 g) carton cottage cheese
salt and pepper
2 oz (50 g) Cheddar cheese, grated

1. Trim leeks, leaving on 3 to 4 inches (7½ to 10 cm) green 'skirt'. Slit. Wash thoroughly. Coarsely chop.
2. Put into pan with potatoes and boiling salted water. Cook, covered, until potatoes are just tender. Strain. Slice potatoes when cool enough to handle.
3. For sauce, melt butter or margarine in pan. Add gammon. Fry until golden brown. Stir in flour. Cook for 1 minute. Gradually blend in cold milk.
4. Cook, stirring, until sauce comes to boil and thickens. Simmer for 2 minutes. Mix in cottage cheese. Season to taste.
5. Fill 3-pint (1¾-litre) well-buttered dish with alternate layers of potatoes, leeks and sauce.
6. Sprinkle top with cheese and reheat and brown for 30 minutes in hot oven set to 210°C (425°F), Gas 7.

Serves 4 to 6

Veal

Martini Veal with Prunes

An unusual and interesting veal dish. Make it during the summer when slim carrots, small potatoes and spring onions are available and at their very best.

2 lb (900 g) stewing veal, diced
1 oz (25 g) flour
2 oz (50 g) butter or margarine
2 tablespoons salad oil
2 bunches of spring onions, trimmed and coarsely chopped
1 garlic clove, crushed
1 lb (450 g) baby new carrots, scraped but left whole
12 large prunes, with stones removed
1 lb (450 g) new potatoes
1 medium orange, sliced
¼ pint (150 ml) dry martini
½ level teaspoon tarragon
2 level teaspoons salt

1. Wash and dry veal and coat with flour. Heat butter or margarine and oil in saucepan. Add veal, spring onions and garlic.
2. Fry fairly briskly until meat is well sealed. Transfer to large greased casserole.
3. Add all remaining ingredients and mix in very well. Cover with lid or foil. Cook for $1\frac{1}{2}$ to $1\frac{3}{4}$ hours in centre of moderate oven set to 180°C (350°F), Gas 4.

Serves 6

Martini Rabbit with Prunes
Make exactly as above but use 6 rabbit joints instead of veal, and soak first in salted water with added lemon juice to remove strong taste.

Hunter's Veal

A lovely old classic, full of piquancy and interest.

1½ lb (675 g) pie veal
1 oz (25 g) butter or margarine
1 tablespoon salad oil
8 oz (225 g) onions, chopped
2 rounded tablespoons tomato purée
½ pint (275 ml) dry white wine
8 oz (225 g) tomatoes, blanched, skinned and chopped
2 level teaspoons salt
1 level teaspoon sugar
1 bouquet garni
1 lb (450 g) potatoes, halved or quartered, depending on size
6 oz (175 g) button mushrooms
2 level tablespoons cornflour
3 tablespoons cold water
3 tablespoons brandy

1. Wash and dry veal. Heat butter or margarine and oil in pan. Add veal. Fry until well sealed and just beginning to turn brown.
2. Move to one side of pan. Add onions. Fry until pale gold. Stir in purée, wine, tomatoes, salt, sugar and bouquet garni.
3. Bring to boil, stirring. Cover. Simmer for 1 hour. Add potatoes. Cover. Simmer for a further 15 minutes. Add mushrooms. Cover again and simmer for 15 to 20 minutes. Remove bouquet garni and discard.
4. To thicken, mix cornflour smoothly with water. Add to veal mixture. Boil, stirring, until bubbly. Heat brandy separately until lukewarm. Flame. Pour over veal and mix in.

Serves 4 to 6

Hunter's Liver
Make exactly as above but use 1 lb (450 g) chicken livers instead of veal and simmer for 45 minutes before adding potatoes.

95

Crunchy Veal in the Pan

A lively way of preparing veal with the appetising crunch of toasted brazil nut slices.

2 lb (900 g) stewing veal (boned weight)
1 oz (25 g) butter or margarine
8 oz (225 g) onions, chopped
1 garlic clove, crushed
½ pint (275 ml) champagne cider
4 oz (125 g) frozen or canned sweetcorn
8 oz (225 g) courgettes, sliced
3 oz (75 g) brazil nuts, thinly sliced and lightly toasted under the grill
2 level teaspoons salt
1 lb (450 g) potatoes, cubed
1 level tablespoon cornflour
2 tablespoons cold water
2 heaped tablespoons chopped parsley or fresh dill

1. Wash and dry veal then cut into 2-inch × 1-inch (5-cm × 2½-cm) strips. Heat butter or margarine in pan. Add veal. Fry until well browned, turning frequently.
2. Add onions and garlic to pan. Continue to fry until pale gold. Pour cider into pan then add sweetcorn, courgettes, 2 oz (50 g) brazil nuts and the salt.
3. Simmer, covered, for 1 hour or until the veal is tender. Mix in potatoes and continue to cook, covered, for a further 20 to 25 minutes or until potatoes are tender.
4. To thicken, mix cornflour smoothly with water. Pour into pan. Bring to boil, stirring. Simmer for 5 more minutes, transfer to a warm serving dish and sprinkle with rest of nuts and either parsley or dill.

Serves 6

Right: Pork Layer Casserole (page 69).

Veal Chop Casserole

A tasty way of preparing veal which enlivens an otherwise mild-tasting bland meat. Serve with baked jacket potatoes.

10 oz (275 g) onions, chopped
1 large leek, trimmed with 2 inches (5 cm) green 'skirt' left on and
*   shredded*
4 oz (125 g) celery, thinly sliced
15 oz (425 g) can red kidney beans, drained
4 veal chops, each about 6 oz (175 g)
1 to 2 level teaspoons salt
½ pint (275 ml) lager
¼ level teaspoon nutmeg

1. Well grease a deep casserole. Cover base with mixture of half the onions, leek, celery and beans.
2. Place chops on top in single layer. Sprinkle with rest of beans and salt then cover with remaining onions, leek and celery.
3. Pour lager carefully into dish, dust top with nutmeg and cover with lid or greased foil. Cook for 1½ hours in moderately hot oven set to 190°C (375°F),Gas 5.

Serves 4

Left: Sausage Paprika (page 83).

Compôte of Veal

A glorious miscellany of veal and vegetables simmered together in sparkling cider, tomato juice and spices.

3 oz (75 g) butter or margarine
2 lb (900 g) stewing or pie veal, diced
8 oz (225 g) onions, chopped
½ pint (275 ml) champagne cider
¼ pint (150 ml) tomato juice
1 level teaspoon soft brown sugar
2 medium leeks, trimmed with 3 inch (7½ cm) green 'skirt' left on, and sliced
1 lb (450 g) mixed root vegetables to include parsnips, swede, carrots and turnip, diced
4 oz (125 g) pumpkin, diced
3 medium celery stalks, sliced
2 to 3 level teaspoons salt
1 bouquet garni
3 level tablespoons cornflour
4 tablespoons cold water
pepper
1½ lb (675 g) peeled potatoes, halved

1. Heat butter or margarine in flameproof casserole. Add veal and onions. Fry until lightly browned for about 20 minutes over low heat.
2. Add cider, tomato juice, sugar, leeks, root vegetables, pumpkin, celery, salt and bouquet garni.
3. Bring to boil. Lower heat and cover pan. Simmer for 1½ hours. Remove bouquet garni. To thicken, mix cornflour smoothly with water. Add to veal mixture. Cook, stirring, until it bubbles. Season to taste with pepper then add potatoes.
4. Cover. Continue to simmer for a further 25 to 30 minutes or until potatoes are cooked. Stir occasionally.

Serves 6

Orchard Veal
with Bacon Dumplings

Already cut-up pie veal is ideal for this all-in-one main course.

2 lb (900 g) pie veal, diced
2 level tablespoons flour
1 oz (25 g) bacon fat or margarine
12 oz (350 g) carrots, each cut lengthwise into 6 strips
6 small onions, peeled but left whole
½ pint (275 ml) chicken stock
1 level teaspoon thyme
1 tablespoon lemon juice
1½ to 2 level teaspoons salt
8 oz (225 g) fresh or frozen broad beans

Dumplings
½ pint (275 ml) milk
½ level teaspoon salt
1 oz (25 g) butter or margarine
4 oz (125 g) semolina
1 level teaspoon mustard powder
1 oz (25 g) self-raising flour
2 Grade 3 eggs
4 oz (125 g) streaky bacon, finely chopped

1. Wash and dry veal then coat all pieces with flour. Heat bacon fat or margarine in heavy pan. Add veal. Fry until well sealed and brown.
2. Add carrots, onions, stock, thyme, lemon juice, salt and beans. Bring to boil, stirring. Cover pan. Lower heat. Simmer for 1¾ hours.
3. After meat has been cooking for 45 minutes, prepare dumplings. Heat milk, salt and butter or margarine slowly until fat melts. Add semolina, mustard and flour.
4. Cook, stirring, until mixture comes to boil and thickens sufficiently to leave sides of pan clean.
5. Beat in eggs and bacon. Cool for about 30 minutes. Drop 6 to 9 dumplings from a wetted spoon on top of veal mixture. Cover. Cook for 15 to 20 minutes or until dumplings are well-puffed.

Serves 6

Veal Chops Mozzarella

Italian style and very appealing, here is a dish designed for devotees of Mediterranean-style cooking. Serve with pasta or rice.

14 oz (400 g) can tomatoes
2 garlic cloves, crushed
1 level teaspoon basil
1 level teaspoon salt
6 oz (175 g) mushrooms, sliced
6 to 7 canned artichoke hearts, drained and quartered
4 tablespoons Marsala
4 veal shops, each about 6 oz (175 g)
1 oz (25 g) butter or margarine, melted (or 1 tablespoon olive oil if preferred)
salt and pepper
8 oz (225 g) Mozzarella cheese, sliced

1. Mash tomatoes and mix with garlic, basil and salt. Arrange over base of a well greased oblong, shallow heatproof dish.
2. Stir in mushrooms, artichoke hearts and Marsala. Add chops, in single layer, on top.
3. Coat with melted butter or margarine (or oil) then season to taste with salt and pepper. Cover with lid or greased foil. Cook for 1 hour in moderate oven set to 180°C (350°F), Gas 4.
4. Uncover. Cover with cheese slices and melt under a hot grill. Serve straight away.

Serves 4

Chicken Mozzarella
Make as above but use 4 chicken joints (breast portions) instead of veal.

Poultry and Game

Chicken in the Swim

An unusual and tasty way of presenting a whole chicken as a main course dish which is ideal for entertaining. Serve with creamed potatoes and fried or grilled tomatoes. (See jacket picture.)

3 lb (1½ kg) oven-ready chicken

Stuffing
4 oz (125 g) fresh brown breadcrumbs
4 oz (125 g) onion, grated
2 oz (50 g) brazil nuts, coarsely chopped
1 level teaspoon salt
2 Grade 3 eggs

To cook
2 rounded tablespoons flour
2 tablespoons salad oil
8 oz (225 g) frozen macedoine of vegetables, partially thawed
¾ pint (425 ml) dry white wine
2 tablespoons mushroom ketchup
1 to 1½ level teaspoons salt
½ level teaspoon dried tarragon

1. Rinse bird inside and out under cold, running water and dry with paper towels.
2. For stuffing, mix all ingredients well together and spoon into body cavity of bird.
3. Coat chicken all over with flour. Heat oil in large, heavy pan. Add chicken. Fry until golden brown all over, turning twice with 2 wooden spoons. Remove to plate.
4. Add vegetables to rest of oil in pan. Fry until warm gold over medium heat, turning from time to time. Stir in all remaining ingredients, including any leftover flour.
5. Bring to boil, stirring, then place chicken on top. Lower heat. Cover. Simmer for 1½ hours. Transfer bird, vegetables and pan juices to a dish. Cut into portions and serve with stuffing.

Serves 4 to 6

Spring Chicken with Apple Juice

Made with apple juice and mixed vegetables, here is a refreshingly different chicken dish for mid-week eating. Creamed potatoes go with it very well. (See illustration facing page 129.)

2 oz (50 g) butter or margarine
2 teaspoons salad oil
4 chicken joints
6 oz (175 g) onions, chopped
1½ oz (40 g) flour
½ pint (275 ml) apple juice
4 tablespoons water
8 oz (225 g) pickling onions or shallots, left whole
8 oz (225 g) carrots, cut into large chunks
8 oz (225 g) fresh peas (weighed after shelling)
parsley for garnish

1. Heat butter or margarine and oil in large pan. Add chicken and fry until joints are golden brown all over, turning twice. Remove to plate.
2. Add onions to pan. Fry over medium heat until light gold. Stir in flour. Cook for 1 minute. Blend in apple juice and water. Bring to boil, stirring.
3. Replace chicken. Add onions and carrots. Cover. Simmer for about 1 hour or until chicken is tender. Mix in peas and continue to cook for a further 25 to 30 minutes or until tender, keeping pan covered and stirring occasionally. Serve garnished with parsley.

Serves 4

Chicken with Grapes and Almonds

A delicious chicken meal made with wine, black grapes and mixed vegetables. Soured cream adds that final touch of gourmet richness. Serve with a green salad tossed with French dressing.

1 oz (25 g) butter or margarine
2 teaspoons salad oil
4 chicken joints cut into pieces
8 oz (225 g) onions, chopped
2 medium celery stalks, sliced
6 oz (175 g) carrots, thinly sliced
1 lb (450 g) potatoes, halved or left whole if small and new
1 bouquet garni
$\frac{1}{4}$ pint (150 ml) chicken stock
$\frac{1}{2}$ pint (275 ml) rosé wine
2 level teaspoons salt
1 oz (25 g) almond flakes, toasted
4 oz (125 g) black grapes, halved with seeds removed
8 oz (225 g) button mushrooms
2 level tablespoons cornflour
2 tablespoons cold water
5 oz (142 ml) carton soured cream

1. Heat butter or margarine and oil in large pan. Add chicken and fry fairly briskly until well browned, turning twice. Remove to plate
2. Add onions, celery and carrots to remaining fat in pan. Fry over medium heat for about 10 minutes or until a warm gold. Replace chicken.
3. Mix in potatoes then add bouquet garni, stock, wine, salt and almonds. Bring to boil, stirring gently.
4. Lower heat and cover. Simmer gently for 45 minutes or until chicken is tender. Add grapes and mushrooms. Simmer for another 10 to 15 minutes, keeping pan covered.
5. To thicken, mix cornflour with water. Pour into pan. Cook until mixture bubbles and thickens, stirring. Finally, blend in cream.

Serves 4

Asparagus Chicken

Extravagantly flavoured and exceptionally good for entertaining. Serve with a green or mixed salad.

1 lb (450 g) potatoes, grated
8 oz (225 g) onions, grated
3 oz (75 g) butter or margarine
1 tablespoon salad oil
8 chicken joints
2 level teaspoons tarragon
2 cans condensed asparagus soup
4 heaped tablespoons fresh brown breadcrumbs or crushed corn-flakes

1. Heat 2 oz (50 g) butter or margarine and oil in pan. Fry chicken joints for about 20 minutes over medium heat, turning from time to time. When ready, the chicken should be a warm gold. Remove to plate.
2. Add vegetables to pan. Fry until golden.
3. Add tarragon then mix in both cans of soup. Bring to boil, stirring. Replace chicken.
4. Lower heat. Cover. Simmer for 45 minutes to 1 hour, or until chicken is tender. Transfer to buttered casserole.
5. Sprinkle with crumbs. Melt rest of butter or margarine and trickle over the top. Brown under a hot grill.

Serves 8

Celery Chicken
For those who prefer the flavour, make as previous recipe but use condensed celery soup instead of asparagus.

Barbecued Chicken

One of those quickly prepared dishes, so useful if you've been out shopping all day and want a meal ready in just about 1 hour. It is fairly spicy and delicious with buttered corn on the cob.

1 can condensed tomato soup
¼ pint (150 ml) boiling water
2 tablespoons malt vinegar
1 tablespoon Worcestershire sauce
1 rounded tablespoon chutney
1 level teaspoon mixed spice
½ level teaspoon paprika
4 chicken joints
8 oz (225 g) onions, sliced
1 lb (450 g) potatoes, halved or quartered, depending on size

1. Mix soup with water, vinegar, Worcestershire sauce, chutney, spice and paprika.
2. Arrange chicken joints, onions, and potatoes carefully in a casserole. Do not pile ingredients on top of each other.
3. Coat with soup mixture. Cover with lid or greased foil. Cook for 1 to 1¼ hours in moderately hot oven set to 190°C (375°F), Gas 5. If potatoes are still a little hard, return casserole to oven for a further 10 to 15 minutes.

Serves 4

Barbecued Lamb

Make exactly as above but use 2 lb (900 g) neck of lamb chops, trimmed of surplus fat.

Cucumber Chicken with Walnuts

One of my favourite recipes is this unusual chicken speciality with its stunning bouquet and a flavour to match.

1 oz (25 g) butter or margarine
2 garlic cloves
1 lb (450 g) unpeeled cucumber, sliced wafer-thin
2 oz (50 g) walnuts, chopped
2 level teaspoons salt
8 oz (225 g) tagliatelle verdi (or use plain ribbon noodles if preferred)
¾ pint (425 ml) dry white wine
1 level teaspoon thyme
6 chicken joints

1. Heat butter or margarine in large deep frying pan. Crush garlic directly into pan. Add cucumber and fry with the garlic until it just begins to turn the palest gold.
2. Add walnuts, 1 teaspoon salt, tagliatelle, wine and thyme. Mix well and bring to boil. Arrange chicken joints on top. Sprinkle with rest of salt. Cover closely. Simmer gently for 45 minutes to 1 hour or until chicken is tender.

Serves 6

Chicken Avocado in the Pan

Delicate avocado adds a special note of colour and distinction to this unusual chicken dish. Serve with a simple green salad.

2 oz (50 g) butter or margarine
4 chicken joints
8 oz (225 g) white part of leek, chopped
3 oz (75 g) flaked almonds
4 oz (125 g) carrots, very thinly sliced
1½ oz (40 g) flour
½ pint (275 ml) milk
¼ pint (150 ml) water
5 tablespoons pale sherry
2 level teaspoons salt
3 oz (75 g) easy-cook long grain rice
1 large, ripe avocado
1 tablespoon lemon juice
6 oz (175 g) tomatoes, blanched, skinned and de-seeded

1. Heat butter or margarine in large frying pan. Add chicken. Fry briskly until golden on both sides. Remove to plate.
2. Add leek to pan with almonds and carrots. Fry over minimal heat until pale gold. Stir in flour. Gradually blend in milk and water.
3. Cook, stirring, until mixture comes to boil and thickens. Blend in sherry, salt and rice. Replace chicken.
4. Cover. Simmer, stirring occasionally, for 1 hour or until tender. Just before serving, peel avocado, cube and sprinkle with lemon juice. Cut tomato flesh into strips. Add both to chicken and heat through briefly—no more than 3 to 4 minutes.

Serves 4

Turkey Avocado in the Pan
Make as previous recipe but use 1 lb (450 g) turkey breast fillet instead of chicken. Cook for 35 to 40 minutes before adding avocado and tomatoes.

Old-Fashioned Chicken Casserole

Unusually flavoured with whisky and thickened with porridge oats, this is one of my special concoctions which I have been making for many years in the height of winter. Bake potatoes in their jackets at the same time but on a higher shelf in the oven.

1 oz (25 g) butter or margarine
4 oz (125 g) lean bacon, chopped
4 oz (125 g) carrots, sliced
8 oz (225 g) onions, chopped
2 oz (50 g) turnip, cubed
2 heaped tablespoons porridge oats
4 chicken joints
1 level teaspoon mixed herbs
1 to 1½ level teaspoons salt
2 tablespoons whisky
½ pint (275 ml) chicken stock

1. Heat butter or margarine in saucepan. Add bacon and all prepared vegetables. Fry gently for 10 to 12 minutes or until pale gold. Stir in oats.
2. Transfer to medium-sized roasting tin or 10-inch (25-cm) square heatproof dish of about 3 to 4 inches (7½ to 10 cm) in depth.
3. Arrange chicken joints on top, skin sides uppermost. Add herbs, salt and whisky to stock. Pour over chicken mixture in dish. Cover with foil. Bake for 45 minutes in moderately hot oven set to 190°C (375°F), Gas 5.
4. Uncover and cook for a further 25 to 30 minutes or until chicken is cooked through and golden.

Serves 4

Winter Chicken

A particular favourite with my own family is this appetising chicken dish which is blissfully easy to prepare and a pleasure to eat.

4 oz (125 g) parsnips, thinly sliced
4 oz (125 g) carrots, thinly sliced
8 oz (225 g) onions, thinly sliced
1 large leek, trimmed with 3 inches (7½ cm) green 'skirt' left on then
  sliced
8 oz (225 g) easy-cook long grain rice
2 level teaspoons salt
8 oz (225 g) can tomatoes
1 level teaspoon tarragon
4 chicken joints
1 teaspoon Worcestershire sauce
1 level teaspoon prepared English mustard
¾ pint (425 ml) boiling water

1. Cover base of medium-sized roasting tin with half the vegetables, then sprinkle with all the rice and 1 teaspoon salt.
2. Cover with rest of vegetables, add tomatoes and juice from can then sprinkle with tarragon. Top with chicken joints, skin sides uppermost.
3. Add Worcestershire sauce and mustard to boiling water then gently pour over chicken in tin. Cover with foil. Cook for 1 hour in moderately hot oven set to 190°C (375°F), Gas 5.
4. Uncover and return to oven. Continue to cook for a further 20 to 30 minutes or until chicken is cooked through and golden brown.

Serves 4

Chicken Stew
with Caramel Onions

A splendid springtime meal, packed full of flavour and goodness.

12 small onions or shallots
1 oz (25 g) butter or margarine
1 oz (25 g) light brown soft sugar
3 lb (1½ kg) chicken joints, skinned, removed from bone and cut into
  small pieces
6 oz (175 g) spring carrots, left whole
4 small spring turnips, left whole
1 lb (450 g) new potatoes, left whole
¼ pint (150 ml) dry white wine
2 level teaspoons salt
2 level tablespoons cornflour
¼ pint (150 ml) whipping cream
½ level teaspoon finely chopped fresh mint or ¼ level teaspoon dried
  mint

1. Cook onions or shallots in boiling salted water for 15 minutes. Drain.
2. Heat butter or margarine and sugar in saucepan. Add onions. Toss thoroughly until well coated then fry gently until golden brown and caramelised.
3. Add chicken and continue to fry until light brown all over. Stir in carrots, turnips, potatoes, wine and salt.
4. Bring to boil and skim. Lower heat. Cover. Simmer gently for 1 hour. To thicken, mix cornflour smoothly with a little cream then stir in remainder.
5. Add to chicken. Cook until it bubbles. Stir in mint. Adjust seasoning to taste.

Serves 4

Rabbit Stew with Caramel Onions

Make exactly as previous recipe but use rabbit joints instead of chicken. To eliminate strong taste, soak the rabbit for 2 hours in salted water to which 2 tablespoons of lemon juice have been added.

111

In-A-Hurry Chicken Pot

A quickly made meal which uses leftover rice and storecupboard ingredients.

3 lb (1½ kg) oven-ready chicken, cut into serving-sized joints
1 can condensed cream of mushroom soup
1 soup can water
1 level tablespoon dried mixed green and red pepper flakes
2 level tablespoons dried sliced onions
1 level tablespoon dried parsley
8 oz (225 g) cooked rice (cooked weight)
1 oz (25 g) almond flakes, toasted

1. Wash chicken and put into large pan with soup, water, pepper flakes, onions and parsley.
2. Bring slowly to boil, stirring all the time. Lower heat and cover. Simmer over medium heat for 1 hour, stirring occasionally.
3. Fork in rice and heat through for about 5 minutes. Transfer to warm serving dish and sprinkle with the almonds.

Serves 4 to 6

Right: Cumberland Sausage Casserole (page 81).

Wine-Braised Chicken with Apricots

An ideal dish for late spring and summer entertaining when baby carrots and new potatoes are at their best. It is delicate, tender and beatifully flavoured.

8 chicken joints
8 heaped teaspoons flour
2 oz (50 g) butter or margarine
1 tablespoon salad oil
4 medium celery stalks, sliced
1 lb (450 g) new carrots
8 oz (225 g) onions, chopped
12 oz (350 g) new potatoes
12 oz (350 g) dried apricots, soaked overnight
1 large lemon, thinly sliced
$\frac{1}{4}$ pint (150 ml) rosé wine
1 level teaspoon tarragon
1 heaped tablespoon chopped parsley
$1\frac{1}{2}$ to 2 level teaspoons salt

1. Wash and dry chicken and coat all over with flour. Heat butter or margarine and oil in large pan.
2. Add chicken joints and fry briskly on both sides until golden brown. Remove to plate.
3. Add celery, whole carrots and onions to pan. Fry over medium heat until golden brown, allowing about 7 to 10 minutes.
4. Mix in potatoes, apricots, lemon slices, wine, tarragon, parsley, salt and any leftover flour.
5. Bring to boil, stirring all the time. Replace chicken. Cover pan. Simmer gently for 1 hour or until cooked, stirring occasionally.

Serves 8

Left: Bacon and Vegetable Casserole (page 84).

New Orleans Jambalaya
with Chicken

A zippy speciality from a region strongly influenced by the cooking of
the French, Spanish and black population.

3 tablespoons salad oil
8 oz (225 g) onions, chopped
2 garlic cloves, chopped
2 large celery stalks, sliced
1 medium green pepper, chopped
12 oz (350 g) raw boned chicken, cut into narrow strips
14 oz (400 g) can tomatoes
$\frac{1}{4}$ level teaspoon Tabasco
1 teaspoon Worcestershire sauce
1 pint (575 ml) boiling chicken stock
8 oz (225 g) easy-cook long grain rice
2 level teaspoons salt

1. Heat oil in pan. Add onions, garlic, celery and green pepper. Fry
   gently for 7 to 10 minutes or until pale gold.
2. Add chicken and fry a little more briskly until well sealed and
   brown. Mix in can of tomatoes (crushing them against side of pan
   with fork), Tabasco, Worcestershire sauce, stock, rice and salt.
3. Bring to boil. Lower heat. Stir and cover. Simmer for 25 minutes or
   until rice grains are plump and tender and have soaked up all
   liquid. Serve straight away.

Serves 4

New Orleans Jambalaya with Pork
Make as above but use pork fillet instead of chicken and cut into thin
shreds before frying.

Pasta Chicken Veronique

Rich and in the haute cuisine bracket—make this speciality and impress your guests.

4 chicken joints, each divided in half
1 level tablespoon cornflour
1½ oz (40 g) butter or margarine
2 teaspoons salad oil
4 oz (125 g) onions, grated
¾ pint (425 ml) dry white wine
1 level teaspoon French mustard
¼ level teaspoon tarragon
1 to 1½ level teaspoons salt
6 oz (175 g) pasta bows or shells
3 tablespoons thick, good quality mayonnaise
5 oz (142 ml) carton soured cream
4 oz (125 g) seedless grapes
1 level tablespoon walnut halves, lightly toasted then finely chopped
1 level tablespoon finely chopped parsley

1. Wash and dry chicken then coat with cornflour. Heat butter or margarine and oil in large pan. Add chicken and fry until crisp and golden all over, turning twice. Remove to plate.
2. Add onions to pan and fry until golden brown. Stir in wine. Bring to boil. Mix in mustard, tarragon and salt. Replace chicken. Simmer for about 30 to 35 minutes or until just tender, keeping pan covered.
3. Add pasta and mix in well. Cover. Continue to cook for a further 20 to 30 minutes or until just tender.
4. Remove chicken to warm serving dish and keep hot. Stir mayonnaise, soured cream and grapes into pan juices and pasta. Spoon mixture over chicken in dish. Sprinkle with walnuts and parsley.

Serves 4

Creamed Chicken
with Corn-n-Beans

A dish which requires the minimum of preparation and attention. It is also one which goes down very well with children as it contains all their favourite things. Serve with jacket potatoes or chips.

8 oz (225 g) frozen or canned sweetcorn
15 oz (425 g) can baked beans in tomato sauce
1 tablespoon tomato ketchup
4 chicken joints or 8 drumsticks
1 can condensed cream of chicken soup
3 heaped tablespoons unsalted peanuts, chopped

1. Tip sweetcorn into greased casserole. Add beans and ketchup. Mix together.
2. Stand chicken joints on top. Coat with soup then sprinkle with nuts.
3. Cover with lid or greased foil. Bake for about 1 hour in moderate oven set to 180°C (350°F), Gas 4. Uncover. Continue to cook for a further 20 to 30 minutes or until top is golden and really crunchy.

Serves 4

Chicken Seville
with Olive Dumplings

Glowing and flavour-packed, this gorgeous chicken dish is afloat with feather-light dumplings. (See illustration facing page 128.)

4 chicken joints
2 level tablespoons flour
1 oz (25 g) butter or margarine
2 tablespoons salad oil
8 oz (225 g) onions, chopped
½ pint (275 ml) Spanish white wine
14 oz (400 g) can tomatoes
2 medium celery stalks, sliced
2 level teaspoons salt

Dumplings
4 oz (125 g) self-raising flour
1 level teaspoon salt
2 oz (50 g) butter or margarine
1 level teaspoon mixed herbs
3 to 4 tablespoons cold milk to mix
8 stuffed olives

1. Cut each chicken joint in to 2 pieces and coat with flour.
2. Heat butter or margarine and oil in flameproof casserole. Add chicken and fry until golden brown and crisp all over, turning twice. Remove to plate.
3. Add onions to pan and fry gently until golden. Replace chicken and any leftover flour. Mix in wine, tomatoes, celery and salt.
4. Cover. Simmer gently for 40 to 45 minutes.
5. For dumplings, sift flour and salt into bowl. Rub in butter or margarine finely. Toss in herbs. Mix to soft dough with milk.
6. Divide into 8 equal portions, shape into dumplings and push an olive into centre of each so that it is completely enclosed.
7. Place dumplings on top of chicken mixture. Cover. Simmer for 20 to 25 minutes or until dumplings are well puffed and double in size.

Serves 4

Chicken Pizzaiola

Typically Italian with a rich vibrant flavour. Serve with a large green salad.

1½ lb (675 g) tomatoes, blanched, skinned and chopped
1 tablespoon salad oil
2 garlic cloves, crushed
2 level teaspoons salt
1 level teaspoon brown sugar
1 rounded teaspoon basil
1 rounded teaspoon thyme
6 chicken joints
4 oz (125 g) elbow or other short macaroni
8 oz (225 g) green beans, sliced
¼ pint (150 ml) Marsala

1. Tip tomatoes into large pan with oil, garlic, salt, sugar, basil and thyme. Bring slowly to boil, stirring. Cover. Simmer for 30 minutes.
2. Add chicken joints and continue to simmer, covered, for about 45 minutes or until tender, stirring occasionally to prevent sticking.
3. Mix in macaroni, beans and Marsala. Cover. Continue to simmer for a further 20 to 30 minutes or until macaroni is just tender.

Serves 6

Pork Chops Pizzaiola
Make exactly as above but use 6 medium pork chops instead of the chicken. Simmer for the same length of time.

Calves' Liver Pizzaiola
Make exactly as above but use 1½ lb (675 g) sliced calves' liver instead of chicken. Simmer for only 25 to 30 minutes or until liver is tender.

Chicken Marengo

A stunning Italian dish. Serve with risotto.

4 chicken joints
flour
1½ oz (40 g) butter or margarine
1 tablespoon salad oil
6 oz (175 g) onions, chopped
2 garlic cloves, crushed
12 oz (350 g) tomatoes, blanched, skinned and chopped
2 oz (50 g) tomato purée
½ pint (275 ml) chicken stock
2 level teaspoons salt
4 rounded tablespoons chopped parsley
4 oz (125 g) button mushrooms
4 tablespoons dry white wine
12 to 16 small black olives

1. Wash and dry chicken. Coat fairly heavily with flour. Heat butter or margarine and oil in pan. When sizzling, add chicken.
2. Fry joints until golden brown all over, turning twice. Remove to plate.
3. Add onions and garlic to pan. Fry until light gold. Stir in tomatoes, purée, stock and salt. Bring to boil, stirring.
4. Replace chicken. Lower heat. Cover. Simmer for 45 minutes. Add rest of ingredients. Cover again. Cook through for 10 minutes.

Serves 4

Chicken Cacciatora
Make exactly as previous recipe but omit parsley, double the amount of mushrooms and replace wine with Marsala.

Neapolitan Chicken

Immensely appetising, colourful and best served with freshly boiled green noodles tossed with butter, grated Parmesan cheese and small black olives.

2 oz (50 g) butter or margarine
2 teaspoons salad oil
4 lb (2 kg) chicken, cut into small joints
8 oz (225 g) onions, chopped
3 garlic cloves, crushed
1 level tablespoon flour
14 oz (400 g) can tomatoes
2 rounded tablespoons tomato purée
1 level tablespoon granulated sugar
1 level teaspoon basil
2 heaped tablespoons finely chopped parsley
12 oz (350 g) courgettes, sliced
1 level teaspoon salt
1 lb (450 g) can artichoke hearts, drained

1. Heat butter or margarine and oil in large pan. Add chicken. Fry fairly briskly until golden brown. Remove to plate.
2. Add onions and garlic to pan. Fry until light gold, allowing about 10 to 15 minutes. Stir in flour. Cook for a further minute.
3. Blend in tomatoes, purée, sugar, basil and parsley. Replace chicken. Bring to boil. Lower heat. Cover. Simmer gently for 45 minutes, stirring occasionally. Mix in courgettes and salt. Cover again. Cook for 15 minutes. Add artichoke hearts and heat through for 7 minutes.

Serves 6 to 8

Neapolitan Veal
Make exactly as above but substitute 3 lb (1½ kg) boned and diced pie veal for the chicken.

Easy Chicken Curry

Another of my favourites, made with the basic 'Wagar' sauce (page 162). It goes especially well with chicken and the addition of peas makes this almost a complete meal in itself. It should be served with freshly cooked rice, sliced bananas sprinkled with lemon juice, and thinly sliced raw onion dusted with chili powder.

1 portion curried sauce 'Wagar' (page 162) defrosted
2 lb (900 g) chicken portions divided up into smallish pieces
5 oz (150 g) natural yogurt
1 level teaspoon salt
4 oz (125 g) frozen peas

1. Spoon sauce into pan. Stir in the chicken, yogurt and salt. Bring to boil, stirring.
2. Lower heat and cover. Simmer for about 45 minutes or until chicken is tender. Add peas and cover.
3. Continue to boil gently for a further 10 minutes, stirring occasionally. Serve very hot.

Serves 4

Chicken Paprika Cream
with Csipetke

A smoothly elegant Hungarian-style chicken dish, traditionally part-nered with tiny home-made dumplings. The csipetke are, in fact, rather like pasta.

4 chicken joints
3 level tablespoons flour, well seasoned with salt and pepper
2 oz (50 g) lard or margarine, or 2 tablespoons salad oil
8 oz (225 g) onions, finely chopped
4 oz (125 g) green pepper, chopped
1½ level tablespoons paprika
¼ pint (150 ml) tomato juice
2 teaspoons lemon juice
1 level teaspoon salt
1 bouquet garni
2 teaspoons Pernod
5 oz (142 ml) carton soured cream

Csipetke
8 oz (225 g) self-raising flour
1 level teaspoon salt
1 heaped tablespoon finely chopped parsley
2 tablespoons cooking oil
1 Grade 3 egg, beaten
3 to 4 tablespoons cold water to mix

1. Wash and dry chicken joints then coat all over with seasoned flour. Heat fat or oil in pan until sizzling.
2. Add chicken. Fry quickly until golden brown, turning once. Remove to plate.
3. Add onions and peppers to pan. Fry more gently until pale gold. Stir in all remaining ingredients except cream.
4. Bring to boil and replace chicken. Cover pan. Lower heat. Simmer gently for 45 minutes to 1 hour or until chicken is tender. Stir from time to time to prevent sticking. Finally, remove bouquet garni before whisking in the cream.
5. Meanwhile prepare 'dumplings'. Sift flour and salt into bowl. Add parsley. Using fork, stir in oil, egg and water to form a stiff dough.

122

6. Knead on floured surface until smooth, then roll out to $\frac{1}{2}$ inch (1$\frac{1}{4}$ cm) thickness. Cut into narrow strips then cut strips into small squares. Refrigerate, uncovered, for 30 minutes. About 10 minutes before the chicken is ready, bring a large pan of salted water to the boil.
7. Add 'dumplings' to the water and cook, uncovered, until they float to the surface, allowing about 5 to 7 minutes. Drain thoroughly.
8. Transfer the chicken to a warm serving dish and surround with the cooked csipetke.

Serves 4

Coq au Vin

Marvellous French classic that costs the earth to eat in a restaurant, but is far less pricy if made at home, even if you use good red wine instead of plonk.

3 lb (1½ kg) chicken joints
1 oz (25 g) butter or margarine
2 tablespoons salad oil
8 oz (225 g) onions, chopped
2 garlic cloves, sliced
8 oz (225 g) back bacon, chopped
¾ pint (425 ml) claret or Hungarian Bull's Blood
3 level tablespoons chopped parsley
1 bouquet garni
2 oz (50 g) shallots or pickling onions, left whole
8 oz (225 g) button mushrooms
2 level tablespoons cornflour
3 tablespoons cold water
2 tablespoons brandy

1. Wash and dry chicken. Heat butter or margarine and oil in large pan. Add chicken. Fry until golden brown and crusty all over. Remove to plate.
2. Add onions, garlic and bacon to pan. Fry until pale gold. Stir in wine and parsley. Bring to boil.
3. Replace chicken. Add bouquet garni and either shallots or pickling onions. Cover. Simmer gently for 45 minutes. Add mushrooms. Cook for a further 15 minutes.
4. To thicken, mix cornflour smoothly with cold water. Add to chicken mixture. Cook, stirring, until mixture bubbles. Pour brandy into small pan. Heat very gently until just warm. Flame. Stir into the Coq au Vin and serve.

Serves 6

Chicken Mexicana

A curious combination of chocolate with chicken is particular to Mexico and this adaptation will appeal to those who enjoy experimenting with off-beat flavours. Serve with rice.

4 chicken joints, each one halved
2 oz (50 g) flour
4 tablespoons salad oil
8 oz (225 g) onions, chopped
1 garlic clove, crushed
4 oz (125 g) green pepper, chopped
4 oz (125 g) tomatoes, blanched, skinned and chopped
½ pint (275 ml) tomato juice
¼ pint (150 ml) water
4 oz (125 g) frozen or canned sweetcorn
1 oz (25 g) plain chocolate
2 level teaspoons salt
1 teaspoon Tabasco (omit if you dislike fire in food!)
4 cloves

1. Wash and dry chicken then coat pieces with flour. Heat oil in pan. Add chicken. Fry fairly briskly until well browned, turning twice. Remove to plate.
2. Add onions, garlic and pepper to pan. Fry slowly until golden, allowing about 10 to 15 minutes. Mix in any leftover flour, then add tomatoes, tomato juice, water, sweetcorn, chocolate and salt.
3. Cook, stirring, until mixture comes to the boil and thickens. Season with Tabasco and cloves. Replace chicken. Cover and simmer for about 1 hour or until tender.

Serves 6

Turkey Mexicana
Make as previous recipe, but, if preferred, use 4 turkey drumsticks (each about 8 oz or 225 g) instead of chicken joints.

Indonesian Spiced Chicken

Anyone who has been to the Far East or, closer to home, to Holland, will doubtless have enjoyed the subtleties of Indonesian food and below is a taster from what the Indonesians familiarly call the rice table.

2 oz (50 g) desiccated coconut
$\frac{1}{4}$ pint (150 ml) boiling water
8 oz (225 g) onions, cut into eighths
3 garlic cloves
1 rounded tablespoon Sambal Manis (hot condiment)
1 heaped tablespoon flaked almonds
3 tablespoons peanut oil
2 level teaspoons turmeric
1 level teaspoon ground coriander
2 teaspoons lemon juice
$\frac{1}{2}$ level teaspoon finely grated lemon peel
8 medium-sized chicken joints
$\frac{1}{2}$ pint (275 ml) chicken stock
1 rounded teaspoon dark brown soft sugar
$1\frac{1}{2}$ level teaspoons salt

1. For coconut milk, mix together coconut and water. Leave to stand for 30 minutes. Strain through fine mesh sieve, pressing coconut against sides. Leave milk on one side for the time being.
2. Put onion, garlic, Sambal Manis and almond into blender goblet or food processor and run machine until mixture forms a purée.
3. Heat oil in pan. Add purée mixture, turmeric, coriander, lemon juice and lemon peel. Fry, stirring, for 10 minutes, keeping heat low.
4. Add chicken joints and mix round and round in the fried mixture. Pour in stock then sprinkle ingredients with sugar and salt.
5. Bring to boil. Cover. Simmer for 1 hour. Add coconut milk. Continue to cook for a further 15 minutes.
6. Serve accompanied with mixed pickles, freshly boiled rice, prawn crackers and the Condiment as given opposite.

Serves 8

Fruited Kashmir Turkey Curry

Pleasurable and without too much fire, this is one of my best curries. Served with Basmati rice, lime pickle and cucumber yogurt Raita (1 medium cucumber thinly sliced, mixed with 5 oz (150 g) natural yogurt and seasoned with salt to taste).

3 lb (1½ kg) turkey breast fillet, cubed
8 oz (225 g) natural yogurt
2 to 4 level tablespoons mild curry powder
2 garlic cloves, crushed
2 level teaspoons salt
4 oz (125 g) unsalted butter
2 oz (50 g) flaked almonds
4 oz (125 g) seedless raisins
3 oz (75 g) dried apricots
12 oz (350 g) onions, chopped
juice of 1 medium lime (lemon can be used if lime is not available)
lime or lemon slices for garnish

1. Wash and dry turkey cubes and place in glass or enamel dish. Stir in yogurt, curry powder, crushed garlic and salt. Cover with cling film and refrigerate for 12 hours, turning about 3 times.
2. Heat butter in heavy pan. Add almonds. Fry gently until just golden. Lift out on to plate. Repeat with raisins and apricots.
3. Add onions to rest of butter in pan and fry gently until pale gold. Stir in drained turkey cubes and continue to fry for 5 minutes over brisk heat.
4. Replace almonds, raisins and apricots then pour in all leftover yogurt mixture with lime juice. Bring to boil, stirring.
5. Cover. Simmer gently for 1 hour, stirring occasionally. Serve straight away, each portion garnished with a slice of lime.

Serves 6 to 8

Left: Spring Chicken with Apple Juice (page 103).

Turkey and Rice Pot

Full of zest and comfortably filling, this is a useful dish to have on standby for any time of year.

> *3 tablespoons salad oil*
> *4 oz (125 g) onions, thinly sliced*
> *4 oz (125 g) red peppers, cut into strips*
> *1 lb (450 g) turkey breast fillets, cut into strips*
> *1 level teaspoon salt*
> *8 oz (225 g) easy-cook long grain rice*
> *$\frac{3}{4}$ pint (425 ml) chicken stock*
> *8 oz (225 g) frozen or canned sweetcorn*
> *$\frac{1}{4}$ pint (150 ml) rosé wine*

1. Heat oil in pan. Add onions and peppers. Fry for about 10 minutes or until pale gold, stirring. Add turkey strips. Continue to fry fairly briskly for a further 5 minutes. Sprinkle in salt.
2. Stir in rice and stock. Bring to boil, stirring. Cover. Lower heat. Simmer for 15 minutes.
3. Mix in corn and wine. Continue to simmer for a further 10 to 15 minutes or until rice grains are separate and fluffy and have soaked up all the liquid.

Serves 4

Gammon and Rice Pot
Make as previous recipe but use 1 lb (450 g) unsmoked gammon, cut into strips.

Mustardy Rabbit

French in style and a treat for those who appreciate rabbit as a change from chicken. It is good served with a green or mixed salad.

8 joints of rabbit
2 tablespoons lemon juice
2 oz (50 g) butter
1 tablespoon salad oil
3 oz (75 g) onions, grated
1½ oz (40 g) flour
½ pint (275 ml) dry white wine
1 level tablespoon French mustard
1 to 1½ level teaspoons salt
2 level teaspoons tomato purée
1 lb (450 g) potatoes, left whole if new or quartered if large
4 oz (125 g) button mushrooms
¼ pint (150 ml) whipping cream
1 oz (25 g) flaked and lightly toasted almonds
1 rounded tablespoon finely chopped parsley

1. Soak rabbit for 2 hours in cold salted water to which the lemon juice has been added. This reduces the strong flavour of the meat.
2. Rinse rabbit and dry. Heat butter and oil in large pan. Add rabbit and fry until well-browned all over, turning twice. Remove to plate.
3. Add onions to remaining butter in pan. Fry for about 5 minutes or until golden. Stir in flour. Gradually blend in wine. Bring to boil, stirring. Add mustard, salt, and purée. Replace rabbit.
4. Mix well. Cover. Simmer for 45 minutes. Add potatoes. Cover. Simmer for a further 20 minutes. Add whole mushrooms and continue to cook for 10 minutes.
5. Blend in cream and heat through. Turn into a warm serving dish and sprinkle with almonds and parsley.

Serves 8

Mustardy Chicken
Make exactly as previous recipe but use 8 small chicken joints instead of rabbit. There is no need to soak them.

Sweet-Sour Duck with Wine

A Chinese-style duck dish, simmered deliciously in wine with apricots, a selection of vegetables and spaghetti rings.

5 lb (about 2¼ kg) duck
8 oz (225 g) onions
12 oz (350 g) red or green peppers
4 medium celery stalks
1 oz (25 g) margarine
1 level tablespoon cornflour
14½ oz (411 g) can apricot halves
½ pint (275 ml) dry red wine
1 tablespoon soy sauce
2 tablespoons wine vinegar
6 oz (175 g) spaghetti rings
1 level teaspoon salt

1. Cut duck into 4 joints with poultry shears or strong kitchen scissors. Carefully ease skin away from flesh then cut off surplus fat. Leave duck aside in a cool place for the time being.
2. Peel and chop onions. Halve and de-seed pepper then cut flesh into strips. Scrub celery and slice.
3. Heat margarine in heavy pan until sizzling. Add prepared vegetables. Fry for about 15 minutes or until soft and light gold.
4. Stir in cornflour, syrup from can of apricots, red wine, soy sauce, vinegar, spaghetti rings and salt.
5. Bring to boil, stirring. Gently stir in apricot halves then add duck portions. Lower heat. Cover.
6. Simmer for about 1½ to 1¾ hours or until duck is tender, stirring from time to time to prevent sticking.

Serves 4

Apple Duck with Red Cabbage

A novel way of preparing duck, well-suited to winter eating and with a lovely sweet-sour tang.

4 lb (2 kg) duck
1½ lb (675 g) red cabbage, shredded
8 oz (225 g) onions, chopped
3 oz (75 g) pearl barley
½ pint (225 ml) apple juice
3 level teaspoons salt
1 garlic clove, crushed
1 tablespoon malt vinegar
1 rounded tablespoon demerara sugar
10 oz (283 g) can whole potatoes, drained

1. Remove skin and surplus fat from duck to prevent a greasy mixture. Wash inside and out. Leave whole.
2. Put all remaining ingredients, except potatoes, into large pan. Stir well to mix. Bring to boil, stirring.
3. Stand duck on top. Lower heat. Cover. Simmer for 1¾ hours. Add potatoes. Heat through for a further 7 minutes.
4. Remove duck from pan and either carve into slices or cut into 4 joints with poultry shears.
5. Arrange cabbage and potato mixture on warm serving dish then stand duck on top. Serve straight away.

Serves 4

Drunken Duck with Chestnuts

An outstanding duck dish for special occasions which is very much in the haute cuisine class. The trick here is to skin the bird before cooking to eliminate greasiness. The chestnuts thicken the sauce adequately, so flour or cornflour are unnecessary.

4 lb (2 kg) oven-ready duck, thawed if frozen
2 oz (50 g) butter or margarine
2 teaspoons salad oil
12 oz (350 g) onions, very thinly sliced
8 oz (225 g) dried chestnuts, soaked overnight and drained
12 oz (350 g) cooking apples, quartered and sliced
½ pint (275 ml) dry cider
1½ level teaspoons salt
6 oz (175 g) mange tout
1½ (675 g) potatoes, quartered or whole if new

1. Cut duck into 4 joints with poultry shears or strong kitchen scissors. Carefully ease skin away from flesh then cut off surplus fat.
2. Heat butter or margarine and salad oil until sizzling in large saucepan. Add duck joints, flesh sides down at first, and fry on both sides until brown, allowing about 10 minutes. Remove to plate.
3. Add onions, chestnuts and apple slices to pan and fry until lightly browned. Pour in cider then add salt and mange tout. Bring to boil, stirring.
4. Replace duck joints then lower heat. Simmer gently for 1¼ hours then add potatoes. Cover again and continue to cook for a further 25 to 30 minutes or until tender.

Serves 4

Peter's Orange Pheasant

During the season, pheasant can taste superb if it is gently braised instead of roasted in the more traditional fashion, and I'm grateful to a very dear friend and skilled hunter for guiding me through this recipe.

brace of pheasant, cleaned
8 oz (225 g) streaky bacon, chopped
2 oz (50 g) butter
8 oz (225 g) onions, chopped
8 oz (225 g) carrots, sliced
4 oz (125 g) parsnip, diced
4 medium celery stalks, sliced
12 oz (350 g) button mushrooms
1 medium orange, peeled and cut into very thin slices
1 rounded tablespoon chunky marmalade
2 rounded tablespoons redcurrant jelly
½ pint (275 ml) tawny port
¼ pint (150 ml) water
2 rounded teaspoons French mustard
2 to 3 teaspoons salt
2 tablespoons fresh lemon juice
3 level tablespoons cornflour
4 tablespoons cold water

1. Instead of plucking birds, strip off skin and all the feathers will come away with it. Divide each bird into 4 joints.
2. Put bacon and butter into pan and fry until bacon is brown and the fat runs. Add pheasant, a few pieces at a time, and fry until well browned. Remove to plate.
3. Add prepared vegetables to pan. Cover. Fry for about 20 minutes or until pale gold, stirring a few times. Mix in orange slices, marmalade, jelly, port, water, mustard, salt and lemon juice.
4. Bring to boil. Replace pheasant. Lower heat. Cover and simmer for about 1¼ hours or until tender. To thicken, mix cornflour with water. Add to pheasant and simmer for 5 minutes, stirring.

Serves 8

Venison Braise
with Feather Dumplings

An elegant and rather sumptuous game dish where the venison is simmered in its own wine marinade and then topped with feathery-light mustard dumplings.

Marinade
8 tablespoons dry red wine
1 tablespoon lemon juice
3 tablespoons salad oil
$\frac{1}{2}$ level teaspoon dried rosemary, crushed between finger and thumb
    to a coarse powder
1 small bay leaf
2 garlic cloves, crushed
2 level teaspoons dark brown soft sugar
1 tablespoon mushroom ketchup
1 level teaspoon salt
2 teaspoons Worcestershire sauce

To cook
$1\frac{1}{2}$ lb (675 g) venison, diced
$\frac{1}{2}$ pint (275 ml) dry red wine
2 medium leeks, sliced
4 large celery stalks, thinly sliced
2 level tablespoons cornflour
3 tablespoons cold water

Dumplings
4 oz (125 g) self-raising flour
1 level teaspoon mustard powder
$\frac{1}{4}$ level teaspoon salt
2 oz (50 g) butter or margarine
3 tablespoons cold water

1. To make marinade, pour wine into glass or enamel dish then stir in lemon juice, oil, rosemary, bay leaf, garlic, sugar, mushroom ketchup, salt and Worcestershire sauce.
2. Stir in venison cubes, tossing round and round in the marinade. Cover. Refrigerate overnight.

3. Tip into saucepan with extra wine, leeks and celery. Bring to boil, stirring. Cover pan. Simmer for $1\frac{1}{2}$ hours.
4. To thicken, mix cornflour smoothly with water. Stir into venison mixture and bring to boil. Lower heat. Cover and cook gently while preparing dumplings.
5. Sift flour, mustard and salt into bowl. Rub in butter or margarine finely. Fork in water to form a fairly soft dough.
6. Shape into 8 dumplings with floured hands and stand on top of venison. Simmer for about 15 minutes or until dumplings are well puffed and cooked through. Remove bay leaf before serving.

Serves 6

Offal

Ox Liver Carbonnade

With a distinctive flavour all its own, this is a winter treat without rival. (See illustration facing page 144).

2 oz (50 g) margarine
8 oz (225 g) onions, chopped
1 garlic clove, crushed
1½ lb (675 g) ox liver
1 level tablespoon flour
½ pint (275 ml) brown ale
1 level tablespoon French mustard
2 level teaspoons each demerara sugar and salt
¼ level teaspoon freshly milled black pepper
2 large slices brown bread, cut into large cubes
1 lb (450 g) potatoes, halved or quartered, depending on size

Topping
5 to 6 slices French bread
1 oz (25 g) butter, melted
extra mustard

1. Heat margarine in pan. Add onions and garlic. Fry until pale gold. Remove from pan. Meanwhile, cube liver and coat with flour.
2. Add liver to pan. Fry until well-sealed and brown. Add onions and all remaining ingredients except potatoes. Mix well.
3. Transfer to casserole. Cover with lid or greased foil. Cook for 1 hour in cool oven set to 160°C (325°F), Gas 3.
4. Add potatoes. Cover. Cook for a further 40 minutes to 1 hour. Before serving, brush slices of French bread with melted butter then spread with mustard. Brown under grill then stand on top of casserole.

Serves 4 to 5

Belgian Beef Carbonnade
Follow recipe for Ox Liver Carbonnade but use 1½ lb (675 g) braising steak instead of liver. Cook for 1¾ hours before adding potatoes.

Best Liver Bake

Cosseted in red wine and layered with stewing pears, I think you will find this liver dish unusual and likely to become a firm favourite. Serve it with broad beans or a mixed salad.

1 lb (450 g) ox liver, thinly sliced
milk
1 oz (25 g) butter or margarine
6 oz (175 g) onions, chopped
2 level tablespoons flour
1 level teaspoon mustard powder
3 medium cooking pears, peeled, halved, cored and cut into thin slices
6 rashers back bacon, de-rinded and coarsely chopped
1 lb (450 g) potatoes, halved or quartered, depending on size
3 level tablespoons cranberry sauce
½ pint (275 ml) dry red wine
2 level teaspoons salt

1. Cover liver with milk. Soak for 1 hour to remove strong flavour. Drain and rinse. Pat dry.
2. Heat butter or margarine in pan. Add onions. Fry gently until pale gold.
3. Coat liver with the flour and mustard, mixed well together. Fill medium-sized casserole with alternate layers of liver, onions, sliced pears and chopped bacon.
4. Place potatoes and cranberry sauce over the top then carefully pour wine into dish.
5. Sprinkle with salt then cover with lid or greased foil. Cook for 1¼ hours in moderate oven set to 180°C (350°F), Gas 4.
6. Uncover. Continue to cook for a further 20 minutes.

Serves 4

Turkey Liver Risotto

Turkey livers are more readily available all the year round than they used to be, and are excellent value for money. They are delicious in this uncomplicated risotto.

2 oz (50 g) butter or margarine
2 teaspoons salad oil
1 lb (450 g) turkey livers
8 oz (225 g) onions, grated
6 oz (175 g) red or green peppers, cut into thin strips
3 medium celery stalks, sliced
6 oz (175 g) cucumber, peeled and diced
8 oz (225 g) easy-cook long grain rice
1 pint (575 ml) boiling water
2 level teaspoons salt
grated Parmesan cheese

1. Heat butter or margarine and oil in pan. Add livers. Fry for about 15 to 20 minutes or until well sealed and brown. Remove to plate.
2. Add prepared vegetables to pan. Fry for 15 to 20 minutes or until light gold. Mix in rice. Cook for 2 minutes. Replace livers.
3. Add water and salt. Bring to boil, stirring twice. Lower heat. Cover. Simmer for 25 minutes or until rice grains are plump and tender and have absorbed all the liquid. Spoon portions on to warm plates and sprinkle with cheese.

Serves 4 to 5

Chicken Livers in
Curry Cream Sauce

Rich and delicate; a fine dish for entertaining.

2 oz (50 g) butter or margarine
2 teaspoons salad oil
1 lb (450 g) chicken livers
8 oz (225 g) onions, chopped
6 oz (175 g) carrots, coarsely grated
1 garlic clove, crushed
4 oz (125 g) fresh spinach leaves, cut into fine shreds
½ level tablespoon mild curry powder
2 level teaspoons garam masala
½ level teaspoon ground cumin
1 level tablespoon flour
½ pint (275 ml) chicken stock
2 level teaspoons salt
5 oz (142 ml) carton soured cream
2 heaped tablespoons chopped parsley

1. Heat butter or margarine and oil in large pan. Add livers. Fry briskly until well sealed and brown. Remove to plate.
2. Add onions, carrots, garlic and spinach to pan. Fry over medium heat for about 15 to 20 minutes or until pale gold. Stir in curry powder, garam masala, cumin and flour.
3. Gradually blend in stock. Bring to boil, stirring. Replace liver. Season with salt. Simmer, covered, for 30 to 40 minutes or until liver is cooked through. Stir occasionally.
4. Add soured cream, little by little, then spoon mixture into a warm serving dish. Sprinkle with parsley.

Serves 6

Succulent Orange Liver

A very special liver and bacon casserole designed for dinner parties.

3 oz (75 g) butter or margarine
2 teaspoons salad oil
8 oz (225 g) back bacon, cut into small squares
12 oz (350 g) onions, sliced
1 lb (450 g) lamb's or pig's liver, cut into 1-inch (2½-cm) cubes
1 slightly rounded tablespoon flour
14 oz (400 g) can tomatoes
finely grated peel and juice of 1 medium orange
3 tablespoons orange flavour liqueur
8 oz (225 g) fresh or frozen sliced green beans
4 oz (125 g) carrots, very thinly sliced
½ to 1 level teaspoon salt
1½ lb (675 g) potatoes, parboiled and sliced
1 level teaspoon paprika

1. Heat 2 oz (50 g) butter or margarine and oil in pan. Add bacon and onions. Cover pan and fry over low heat for 15 minutes or until tender and just beginning to turn golden.
2. Wash and dry liver. Coat with flour. Add to pan. Fry fairly briskly until well sealed and brown. Stir in tomatoes, orange peel and juice, liqueur, beans, carrots and salt. Bring to boil, stirring.
3. Transfer to large casserole then cover top with overlapping rings of potato slices. Melt rest of butter or margarine and brush over the potato. Sprinkle with paprika.
4. Bake for 1 to 1¼ hours in oven set to 180°C (350°F), Gas 4, when topping should be deep golden in colour.

Serves 4

On-the-spot Liver Casserole

A quick and convenient way of preparing liver, which tastes delicious. Cans provide the short cuts, invaluable for those occasions when time is short.

1 lb (450 g) lamb's or pig's liver, thinly sliced
3 tablespoons milk
2 level tablespoons cornflour
1 oz (25 g) butter or margarine
3 oz (75 g) streaky bacon, chopped
1 large can new potatoes, drained
4 oz (125 g) frozen peas
6 tablespoons boiling water
1 can condensed cream of mushroom soup

1. Wash and dry liver then dip in milk. Coat with cornflour and leave to stand for 5 minutes.
2. Heat butter or margarine in flameproof casserole. Mix in bacon. Fry gently until well browned. Add liver slices, a few pieces at a time.
3. Fry until crisp and golden on both sides, turning twice. Remove from heat. Add potatoes and peas.
4. Mix water into soup. When smooth and evenly blended, pour over ingredients in casserole.
5. Cover. Cook for 40 minutes in moderate oven set to 190°C (375°F), Gas 5.

Serves 4 to 6

Right: Ox Liver Carbonnade (page 139).

Scandinavian Liver Pudding

Beloved in parts of Scandinavia, this slightly sweet pudding is a super way of presenting liver, though I admit it is very much an acquired taste. But try it and see what you think—we love it at home and I often make it. Serve with boiled potatoes.

6 oz (175 g) round grain rice (type suitable for milk puddings)
½ pint (275 ml) boiling water
1 pint (575 ml) milk
2 level teaspoons salt
4 oz (125 g) onions, grated
1 oz (25 g) butter or margarine
1 lb (450 g) lamb's or pig's liver, minced
2 rounded tablespoons golden syrup
3 oz (75 g) seedless raisins
1 level teaspoon marjoram
3 Grade 3 eggs, beaten
cranberry sauce for serving

1. Put rice into heavy saucepan with water, milk and salt. Bring to boil and at once lower heat. Stir round and cover. Simmer very slowly until rice is soft and has absorbed most of the liquid. Allow plenty of time.
2. Fry onions gently in the butter or margarine until light gold. Add to rice mixture with liver, syrup, raisins, marjoram and eggs.
3. Pour into large, well-greased square casserole or medium-sized roasting tin. Cover with lid or greased foil. Cook for 1 hour in slow oven set to 160°C (325°F), Gas 3.
4. Uncover. Continue to cook for a further 45 minutes to 1 hour or until mixture is firm and set.
5. Spoon out of dish or tin on to warm plates and top each with a little cranberry sauce.

Serves 8

Left: Haddock and Cider Casserole (page 157).

Sizzling Kidneys in Red Wine

For those who appreciate the distinctive taste and texture of ox kidneys, this recipe should go down very well indeed as a rather special main course. Grilled or fried mushrooms and tomatoes make an excellent accompaniment.

1 oz (25 g) butter or margarine
6 oz (175 g) onions, chopped
1½ lb (675 g) ox kidney
2 level tablespoons flour
½ pint (275 ml) dry red wine
1½ level teaspoons salt
1 level teaspoon mixed herbs
2 level teaspoons prepared continental mustard
2 teaspoons Worcestershire sauce
1 level tablespoon tomato purée
2 level teaspoons dark brown soft sugar
1 lb (450 g) potatoes, halved or quartered, depending on the size

1. Heat butter or margarine in pan. Add onions. Fry for about 7 to 10 minutes or until golden.
2. Meanwhile, wash and dry kidney. Remove fat and gristle from centre, dice and add to pan, a few pieces at a time. Fry over fairly brisk heat until well sealed and brown, turning.
3. Mix in flour thoroughly. Gradually blend in wine. Cook, stirring, until mixture comes to boil and thickens.
4. Add salt, herbs, mustard, Worcestershire sauce, tomato purée and sugar. Stir in thoroughly. Cover. Simmer for 45 minutes.
5. Stand potatoes on top of kidney mixture. Continue to cook, covered, for a further 25 to 30 minutes or until potatoes are tender.

Serves 4

Cider Liver

Devotees of piquant liver and cider combinations will applaud this recipe and doubtless come back for more.

2 oz (50 g) butter
2 teaspoons salad oil
2 garlic cloves, crushed
1 lb (450 g) thinly sliced lamb's liver
1 level tablespoon flour
½ pint (275 ml) dry cider
4 oz (125 g) frozen or canned sweetcorn
4 oz (125 g) fresh or frozen sliced green beans
¼ pint (150 ml) tomato and vegetable juice (such as V8)
1 level teaspoon soft brown sugar
2 medium tomatoes, blanched, skinned and chopped
2 level teaspoons salt
1 level teaspoon basil

1. Heat butter and oil in pan. Add garlic and slices of liver. Fry until brown and well sealed on both sides. Stir in flour then blend in cider.
2. Bring to boil, stirring. Add sweetcorn, beans, vegetable juice, sugar, tomatoes, salt and basil. Cover. Simmer for 1 hour, stirring occasionally.

Serves 4

Orange Kidneys with Madeira

Elegant and sophisticated, this makes a superb main course cooked with peas and potatoes.

1¼ lb (575 g) pig's or ox kidney
1 pint (575 ml) water
1 tablespoon lemon juice
2 teaspoons salad oil
1 oz (25 g) butter or margarine
6 oz (175 g) onions, chopped
1 level tablespoon flour
¼ pint (150 ml) beef stock
juice of 1 large orange
2 level teaspoons salt
5 tablespoons Madeira
1 level teaspoon brown sugar
8 oz (225 g) peas
1 lb (450 g) peeled potatoes, cubed

1. Dice kidney and soak for 1 hour in water to which lemon juice has been added. This reduces the strong flavour which some people dislike. Drain and wipe dry.
2. Heat oil and butter or margarine in pan. Add onions. Fry over medium heat for about 15 minutes or until golden brown, stirring occasionally. Move to one side of pan. Add diced kidney and fry a little more briskly until well sealed and brown.
3. Stir in flour. Cook for 2 minutes then gradually blend in stock and orange juice. Bring to boil, stirring.
4. Add salt, Madeira and sugar. Cover. Simmer fairly gently for 45 minutes or until kidneys are just tender. Stir occasionally. Mix in peas and potatoes. Continue to simmer for a further 20 to 25 minutes or until potatoes are cooked.

Serves 4

Oxtail Stew

Rich, warming and with a distinctive flavour, little can be better to come home to in mid-winter than this delicious oxtail stew.

$2\frac{1}{2}$ lb (just over 1 kg) oxtail, divided into pieces
2 oz (50 g) margarine or dripping
1 tablespoon salad oil
12 oz (350 g) each onions and carrots, sliced
4 oz (125 g) turnip, sliced
4 oz (125 g) swede, diced
8 oz (225 g) pumpkin, de-seeded and diced
1 bouquet garni
1 pint (575 ml) water
2 level teaspoons salt
1 lb (450 g) potatoes, halved or quartered, depending on size
2 level tablespoons flour
4 tablespoons cold water
3 teaspoons malt vinegar
salt and pepper
1 heaped tablespoon chopped parsley

1. Wash oxtail and dry. Heat margarine or dripping in large pan. Add oxtail. Fry briskly until well browned, turning two or three times. Remove to plate.
2. Add prepared vegetables to rest of fat and oil in pan. Fry, covered, for about 20 minutes. Add bouquet garni, water and salt.
3. Bring to boil, stirring. Replace oxtail. Cover. Simmer for $2\frac{1}{2}$ hours or until tender. Add potatoes. Continue to cook for another 20 to 30 minutes. Cool. Cover. Refrigerate overnight.
4. Next day, remove hard layer of fat from the top. Reheat until boiling. Then, to thicken, mix flour very smoothly with water and vinegar. Add to boiling oxtail. Cook, stirring, until mixture bubbles and thickens. Simmer gently for 10 minutes. Adjust seasoning.
5. Remove bouquet garni and transfer oxtail to warm serving dish. Sprinkle with parsley and serve straight away.

Serves 4

Tripe Provençale

As a change from tripe and onions, this more flavourful rendering should prove popular. Try serving it with slices of fried bread.

2 lb (900 g) dressed tripe
1½ pints ($\frac{7}{8}$ litre) water
2 level teaspoons salt
2 oz (50 g) butter or margarine
2 tablespoons salad oil
12 oz (350 g) onions, chopped
8 oz (225 g) green pepper, chopped
1 garlic clove, chopped
4 oz (125 g) easy-cook long grain rice
½ pint (275 ml) red wine
1 bouquet garni
3 level tablespoons tomato purée
salt and pepper
8 oz (225 g) button mushrooms, thinly sliced

1. Put well-washed tripe into large pan. Add water. Bring to boil and skim. Lower heat and cover pan. Simmer for about 35 to 45 minutes or until tender. Drain. Cut into squares. Leave to drip through colander to remove as much liquid as possible.
2. Heat butter or margarine and oil in saucepan. Add onions, green pepper and garlic. Fry over medium heat until pale gold. Add rice. Fry for a further 5 minutes.
3. Replace tripe then pour wine into pan. Add bouquet garni and tomato purée then season to taste. Bring to boil. Lower heat. Cover. Simmer very gently for 45 minutes, stirring occasionally.
4. Add mushrooms and continue to simmer for a further 10 to 15 minutes. Adjust seasoning to taste and remove bouquet garni bag before serving.

Serves 4

Fish

Eastern Haddock

All too often one overlooks the fact that fish, despite its tenderness, makes a splendid casserole. This one, with its spicy yogurt topping, is an admirable and sophisticated party dish.

8 oz (225 g) easy-cook long grain rice
1 pint (575 ml) boiling water
2 level teaspoons salt
2 level teaspoons garam masala
2 tablespoons salad oil
8 oz (225 g) onions, chopped
1 garlic clove, crushed
1 level teaspoon turmeric
1 level teaspoon paprika
½ level teaspoon ginger
½ level teaspoon cinnamon
1 heaped tablespoon mango chutney
2 medium bananas
1½ lb (675 g) haddock fillet, skinned and flesh cut into strips
12 oz (350 g) natural yogurt
1 heaped teaspoon sesame seeds
1 oz (25 g) butter or margarine, melted

1. Cook rice in water with salt and garam masala for 20 to 25 minutes, or until rice grains are dry and separate and have absorbed all the liquid.
2. Meanwhile, heat oil in pan. Add onions and garlic. Fry for about 15 minutes over medium heat until light gold.
3. Fork in rice, turmeric, paprika, ginger, cinnamon and chutney. Spread over base of fairly shallow, well-buttered heatproof dish.
4. Slice bananas directly over the rice mixture then add a layer of haddock strips. Coat with yogurt, sprinkle with sesame seeds and trickle butter or margarine over the top.
5. Bake, uncovered, for 30 minutes in moderately hot oven set to 200°C (400°F), Gas 6.

Serves 6

Potato and Haddock Layer

A rather delicious mix of goodness, quite happy to take care of itself in the oven. It is good eaten with a large mixed salad or cooked leaf spinach mixed with butter. Or you may like to serve a mixed vegetable platter of cooked cauliflower, carrots, green beans and marrow.

2 lb (900 g) potatoes
1 oz (25 g) butter or margarine
8 oz (225 g) onions, chopped
8 oz (225 g) smoked haddock fillet, cooked in a little water for 10
minutes and then flaked (skin and bones discarded)
2 Grade 3 eggs
¼ pint (150 ml) milk
1 level teaspoon salt
4 oz (125 g) Cheddar cheese, grated

1. Halve large potatoes and leave small ones whole. Cook in boiling salted water until tender. Drain and slice.
2. Heat butter or margarine in pan. Add onions. Fry until pale gold, allowing about 10 to 15 minutes. Stir in cooked haddock and fry for a further 3 minutes.
3. Cover a 2½-pint (1½-litre) buttered heatproof dish with one third of the potato slices. Add half the onion and fish mixture then cover with another third of potatoes. Spread with rest of onion and fish mixture then finally add a single layer of remaining potatoes.
4. Beat eggs, milk and salt well together. Pour into dish. Sprinkle with cheese. Reheat and brown for 45 minutes in a moderately hot oven set to 200°C (400°F), Gas 6.

Serves 4 to 5

Sweetcorn and Smoked Haddock Chowder

Adapted from a North American recipe, chowder is a soup-in-a-plate meal based on milk. It is nourishing and quick and easy to make.

1 oz (25 g) butter or margarine
8 oz (225 g) onions, chopped
2 large scrubbed celery stalks, thinly sliced
1 lb (450 g) potatoes, cut into large cubes
¼ pint (150 ml) chicken stock
8 oz (225 g) cooked sweetcorn
8 oz (225 g) smoked haddock, cooked in a little water for 10 minutes
*   and then flaked (with skin and bones discarded)*
1 pint (575 ml) milk
salt and pepper
3 oz (75 g) Cheddar cheese, grated
chopped parsley for garnish

1. Heat butter or margarine in pan. Add onions and celery. Fry gently for about 10 minutes or until light gold.
2. Add potatoes and stock. Bring to boil, stirring. Lower heat. Cover. Simmer for 15 to 20 minutes or until potatoes are tender, taking care not to overcook.
3. Mix in sweetcorn, haddock and milk. Bring just up to boil and remove from heat. Season to taste then add cheese and stir until melted.
4. Ladle into deep soup bowls or plates and sprinkle with parsley.

Serves 4

Smoky Fish and Bacon Casserole

An unusual blend which makes for an intriguing all-in-one dish with a subtle flavour. Serve with a mixed salad.

6 oz (175 g) streaky bacon
1½ lb (675 g) smoked cod fillet
8 oz (225 g) macaroni
2 oz (50 g) walnuts, very finely chopped
1 garlic clove, crushed
pepper
2 Grade 3 eggs
¼ pint (150 ml) single cream
2 heaped tablespoons crushed bran flakes
1 oz (25 g) butter, melted

1. Chop bacon coarsely and fry in its own fat until crisp and golden. Poach cod fillet in unsalted water until tender, allowing between 10 and 12 minutes, depending on thickness. Drain and flake flesh, discarding skin and bones.
2. Cook macaroni in boiling salted water for no more than 7 to 10 minutes. Drain. Return to pan. Stir in bacon (plus fat) flaked fish, walnuts, garlic and pepper to taste.
3. Beat together eggs and cream. Add to fish mixture and toss well with two spoons. Transfer to well-buttered, fairly shallow heat-proof dish.
4. Sprinkle with crushed bran flakes then trickle butter over the top. Bake, uncovered, until piping hot and golden, allowing about 20 to 25 minutes in hot oven set to 210°C (425°F), Gas 7.

Serves 6

Southern Fish Hotpot

Full of taste, this is a novel way of presenting fish and quite delicious.
Mange tout or freshly cooked peas tossed in butter make an excellent
accompaniment.

> 2 tablespoons salad oil
> 8 oz (225 g) onions, chopped
> 1 lb (450 g) tomatoes, blanched, skinned and chopped
> 3 rounded tablespoons tomato purée
> 8 oz (225 g) courgettes, sliced
> 2 teaspoons lemon juice
> 2 level teaspoons soft brown sugar
> 1 level teaspoon basil
> 1 level teaspoon salt
> 1½ lb (675 g) skinned haddock fillet, cut into large cubes
> 3 oz (75 g) button mushrooms, halved
> 1 lb (450 g) cooked potatoes, sliced
> 3 oz (75 g) Cheddar cheese, finely grated

1. Heat oil in pan. Add onions. Fry over medium heat until pale gold.
   Add tomatoes, purée, courgettes, lemon juice, sugar, basil and salt.
2. Bring to boil, stirring. Lower heat. Cover. Simmer for 15 minutes.
   Stir in haddock and mushrooms. Transfer to a shallow heatproof
   dish, or a medium-sized roasting tin.
3. Cover top with bands of overlapping slices of potatoes then
   sprinkle with cheese. Cook for 30 to 40 minutes in moderately hot
   oven set to 200°C (400°F), Gas 6.
4. When ready, the potato topping should be a warm golden brown
   and the fish cooked through.

Serves 4 to 6

Haddock and Cider Casserole

A healthy dish which is low in calories and interestingly flavoured. (See picture facing page 145.)

8 oz (250 g) onions, finely chopped
4 oz (125 g) mushrooms, sliced
1 can (14 oz or 400 g) tomatoes, drained
1 rounded tablespoon chopped parsley
1 level teaspoon basil
2 level tablespoons flour
1½ lb (675 g) haddock fillet, skinned
salt and pepper
¼ pint (125 ml) dry cider
3 oz (75 g) wholemeal breadcrumbs
4 oz (125 g) Edam cheese, grated

1. Put the onion, mushrooms and tomatoes into a 3 pint (1½ litre) greased casserole. Sprinkle with herbs and flour.
2. Divide the fish into four portions, season with salt and pepper and roll up. Place on top of vegetable mixture. Pour over cider.
3. Mix together breadcrumbs and cheese. Sprinkle over fish. Bake, uncovered, for 35 minutes in a moderate oven set to 180° C (350° F) Gas 4.

Serves 4

Bouillabaisse

A soup which is a meal in itself from the French Mediterranean, served with hunks of crusty bread and a hot relish called Rouille. The Bouillabaisse and the relish take a bit of time to make, but the result is well worth the effort.

1 pint (575 ml) dry white wine
2½ pints (1½ litres) water
2 bouquet garni
1 lb (450 g) white fish trimmings to include bones
3 cloves
3 level teaspoons salt
12 oz (350 g) tomatoes
1 large onion, quartered
1 garlic clove, sliced
1½ lb (675 g) plaice, sole or halibut fillets, skinned
12 oz (350 g) peeled prawns
1 lb (450 g) fresh mussels, cleaned

1. Put wine, water, bouquet garni bags, fish trimmings, cloves, salt, tomatoes, onion and garlic into pan. Bring to boil. Lower heat. Cover. Simmer gently for 1½ hours. Strain.
2. Return to clean pan. Cut fish into fairly large pieces and add to the pan. Bring to boil. Simmer for 5 minutes. Add prawns and mussels. Cover. Simmer for a further 5 minutes.
3. Ladle into deep soup plates and top each with Rouille.

Serves 8

Rouille

6 oz (175 g) green pepper, halved
1 teaspoon Tabasco sauce
½ (275 ml) water
2 pickled red peppers, from jar or can
2 garlic cloves
6 tablespoons salad oil
crumbs from 2 large slices brown bread
salt

1. Mince or very finely chop green pepper. Tip into bowl. Add Tabasco and water. Very finely chop the pickled peppers and the garlic.
2. Add to green pepper mixture with oil, crumbs and salt to taste.
3. Rouille should be consistency of chutney. If too thick, thin down with some of the liquid from the Bouillabaisse; if too thin, add a few more crumbs.

Serves 8

Vegetables,
Cheese and Eggs

Hungarian Mushrooms

Imagine a vegetable and egg goulash laced with cream and wine for mid-week eating! It's economical and cooks in next to no time.

3 oz (75 g) butter or margarine
1 tablespoon salad oil
1½ lb (675 g) button mushrooms
12 oz (350 g) onions, chopped
2 garlic cloves, thinly sliced
1 rounded tablespoon paprika
1 level tablespoon flour
2 level tablespoons tomato purée
¼ pint (150 ml) each red wine and water
1 large red or green pepper, cut into strips
8 oz (225 g) tomatoes, blanched, skinned and chopped
¼ level teaspoon caraway seeds
1 level teaspoon marjoram
2 level teaspoons salt
white pepper
4 oz (125 g) pasta shells
5 oz (142 ml) carton soured cream
6 Grade 3 eggs, hard-boiled

1. Heat butter or margarine and oil in large pan until sizzling. Add mushrooms. Fry briskly for 2 minutes, turning frequently. Remove.
2. Add onions and garlic to pan. Fry gently for about 10 minutes or until just beginning to turn a rich golden colour.
3. Stir in paprika, flour, purée, wine, water, peppers, tomatoes, caraway seeds, marjoram, salt and pepper to taste. Replace mushrooms.
4. Bring to boil, stirring. Lower heat. Cover. Simmer over medium heat for 10 minutes. Mix in pasta. Continue to cook for a further 20 minutes or until tender.
5. Keep pan covered and stir at least twice during cooking. Blend in cream, add whole shelled eggs and warm through for 5 minutes.

Serves 6

Vegetable Curry `Wagar´

An authentic, home-made 'cook-in' curry sauce for curry addicts which was kindly given to me by the owner of Vijay's Food Store in Chatham, Kent. It can be used for meat, poultry, eggs and vegetables. Because it deep freezes so perfectly, I have given quantities for four batches of cook-in sauce, each of which can be used on separate occasions. The sauce is the basis for this vegetable curry and for the pork, egg and chicken curries included elsewhere in the book, but I must add that some of the ingredients are available only from Oriental shops—they do need seeking out.

Sauce
8 tablespoons salad oil
1 level teaspoon black mustard seeds
3 cinnamon sticks, each 2 to 3 inches (5 to 7½ cm) in length
1 rounded teaspoon cumin seeds
12 cloves
1¼ lb (575 g) onions, chopped
2 garlic cloves
½ oz (15 g) fresh ginger
3 to 12 medium-sized, fresh green chilis (depending on how hot you like your curry)
3 × 14 oz (400 g) cans tomatoes
2 rounded tablespoons ground cumin
2 rounded tablespoons ground coriander
1 rounded tablespoon turmeric
1 level teaspoon cinnamon
3 rounded teaspoons salt

Vegetable Mixture
8 oz (225 g) potatoes, diced
6 oz (175 g) onions, diced
4 oz (125 g) carrots, thinly sliced
4 oz (125 g) green cabbage, coarsely shredded
¼ pint (150 ml) water
1 level teaspoon salt

1. For sauce, heat oil until sizzling in large and heavy pan. Add mustard seeds. Cover pan. Cook until you can hear them pop—2 to 3 minutes.
2. Add cinnamon sticks, cumin seeds and cloves. Fry gently, covered, for 5 minutes.
3. Add onions. Using garlic crusher, crush garlic directly into pan. Repeat with the peeled ginger which is no harder to crush than garlic and certainly easier than chopping. Mix well.
4. Fry gently while preparing chilis. Wash and dry. Slit lengthwise then carefully remove and discard seeds as these are very fiery. Ensure that none comes into contact with your eyes or mouth and it is advisable to scrub your hands thoroughly after handling.
5. Cut chilis into strips (not too thin) and add to pan. Fry all ingredients slowly until golden brown, stirring from time to time.
6. Add cans of tomatoes and all remaining ingredients. Crush tomatoes against sides of pan and then stir well to mix. Simmer for 10 minutes. Divide into 4 equal parts. Deep-freeze 3 parts (separately for convenience) when cold.
7. To make vegetable curry, tip fourth portion of sauce into pan. Stir in vegetables, water and salt.
8. Bring to boil, stirring. Simmer over medium heat until vegetables are tender, allowing about 30 minutes.
9. Stir from time to time to prevent sticking. Serve very hot with the accompaniments below to give you a complete meal.

Accompaniments
Lime pickle, mango chutney, a small dish of chopped salted peanuts and freshly cooked rice.

Serves 4

Egg and Spinach Curry

Made with the curry sauce 'Wagar' (page 162), this is a very easy, high-speed curry. Serve with rice and chutney.

> *1 portion curried sauce 'Wagar' (page 162), defrosted*
> *8 oz (225 g) frozen chopped spinach*
> *1 rounded tablespoon desiccated coconut*
> *5 oz (142 ml) carton soured cream*
> *1 level teaspoon salt*
> *8 Grade 3 hard-boiled eggs, freshly cooked*
> *2 large tomatoes, blanched, skinned and chopped*

1. Spoon sauce into pan. Add spinach and coconut. Bring to boil, stirring. Lower heat. Cover.
2. Simmer gently until spinach has completely melted, and mixture is bubbling. Season to taste with salt.
3. Shell eggs, leave whole and add to sauce with tomatoes. Heat through for about 7 to 10 minutes. Serve straight away.

Serves 4

Brunch in a Pot

Just the thing for brunch on Sunday—that late breakfast early lunch, borrowed from America. It's quick, tasty and needs few additions.

1 lb (450 g) potatoes, halved or quartered, depending on size
4 Grade 3 eggs, hard-boiled
6 oz (175 g) Lancashire cheese, crumbled
salt and pepper
½ pint (275 ml) milk
6 oz (175 g) tomatoes, sliced

1. Cook potatoes in boiling salted water for 10 minutes. Drain. Rinse under cold water. Slice.
2. Shell eggs and slice. Fill greased casserole with alternate layers of potatoes, eggs and 4 oz (125 g) cheese, finishing with potatoes and sprinkling salt and pepper between layers.
3. Pour milk into dish then arrange tomatoes on top. Sprinkle with rest of cheese and cook, uncovered, for 30 to 35 minutes in moderately hot oven set to 200°C (400°F), Gas 6.

Serves 4

Brunch in a Mushroom Pot

For those who don't take kindly to eggs, follow the above recipe but substitute 8 oz (225 g) sliced and fried mushrooms for the eggs.

Chicory Braise with Eggs

A distinctive speciality, based on Belgian chicory and particularly attractive to vegetarians.

3 heads of chicory
1½ oz (40 g) butter or margarine
8 oz (225 g) onions, chopped
1½ lb (675 g) potatoes, diced
2 level teaspoons salt
1 tablespoon fresh lemon juice
¼ level teaspoon tarragon
½ teaspoon Worcestershire sauce
4 tablespoons water
4 freshly-fried eggs

1. Remove the triangular shaped 'core' from the base of each head of chicory as this reduces bitterness. Take off and discard any bruised outer leaves. Slice.
2. Heat butter or margarine in pan. Add onions and fry until golden. Add chicory and potatoes with rest of ingredients except eggs.
3. Cover. Simmer very gently over minimal heat allowing about 15 to 20 minutes. Stir frequently. Pile on to 4 warm plates and top each with a fried egg.

Serves 4

Courgettes Braise with Eggs
Follow previous recipe but, if preferred, use 1 lb (450 g) sliced courgettes instead of chicory.

Party Rice and Lentil Curry with Eggs

Mild yet with a subtle taste and aroma, this is a curry I find myself making quite often for parties. Not only is it a meal by itself, but it is also delicious with hard-boiled eggs; well worth trying.

3 tablespoons salad oil
8 oz (225 g) red and yellow peppers, cut into strips
6 oz (175 g) onions, chopped
1 garlic clove, sliced
4 oz (125 g) celery, sliced
8 oz (225 g) easy-cook long grain rice
8 oz (225 g) orange lentils
2 × 14 oz (400 g) cans tomatoes
4 to 8 rounded teaspoons Madras curry powder (according to taste)
1 rounded teaspoon ground cumin
1½ pints (⅞ litre) boiling water
3 to 4 level teaspoons salt
1 rounded tablespoon lime pickle
8 to 12 Grade 3 eggs

1. Heat oil in large pan. Add peppers, onions, garlic and celery. Fry over medium heat, with lid on pan, for about 15 minutes or until pale gold.
2. Stir in all remaining ingredients. Bring to boil stirring. Lower heat. Cover. Cook for about 30 to 40 minutes or until rice is tender and most of the liquid has been absorbed.
3. About 15 minutes before curry is ready, hard boil the eggs then shell and halve lengthwise. Arrange curry in a large, warm serving dish and top with egg halves, yolk sides uppermost. Serve straight away.

Accompaniments
Lime pickle, mango chutney, cut-up tomatoes sprinkled with French dressing, sliced onion rings lightly sprinkled with fresh chopped coriander or parsley.

Serves 8 to 10

Mushroom and Pasta Hotpot

Rich, appetising and economical; a dish well worth holding in reserve when you fancy a meatless day. Serve with a green salad or green vegetable.

2 oz (50 g) butter
2 teaspoons salad oil
8 oz (225 g) onions, chopped
12 oz (350 g) mushrooms, sliced
6 oz (175 g) pasta shells, parboiled for 5 minutes
3 Grade 2 eggs
5 oz (142 ml) carton soured cream
2 level teaspoons salt
1 level teaspoon French mustard
8 oz (225 g) tomatoes, sliced
2 oz (50 g) Edam cheese, grated
paprika

1. Heat butter and oil in large pan. Add onions and mushrooms. Fry over medium heat for about 7 minutes or until just beginning to turn golden.
2. Spread half the pasta over buttered 3-pint (1¾-litre) heatproof dish. Cover with mushroom mixture and sprinkle rest of pasta on top.
3. Beat eggs thoroughly with cream, salt and mustard. Pour into dish over pasta then top with a border of tomato slices.
4. Sprinkle with cheese and paprika. Cook for 40 minutes in moderately hot oven set to 190°C (375°F), Gas 5.

Serves 4 to 6

Jansson's Temptation

A Swedish classic which, the story goes, was the downfall of a man of the cloth called Erik Jansson who was unable to resist the succulence of this glorious potato dish, enriched with cream. Serve with a mixed salad.

2 lb (900 g) potatoes
12 oz (350 g) onions, very thinly sliced
about 1½ oz (40 g) can anchovies in oil, drained and coarsely chopped (reserve oil)
¾ pint (425 ml) whipping cream
1 oz (25 g) butter, melted

1. Grate potatoes. Use half to cover base of well buttered, shallow oblong heatproof dish.
2. Top with layers of half the onion slices, all the anchovies, rest of onions and finally remaining potatoes.
3. Coat with half the cream then trickle butter and anchovy oil over the top. Bake, uncovered, for 20 minutes in a moderately hot oven set to 200°C (400°F),Gas 6.
4. Pour over the remaining cream and bake, again uncovered, for a further 30 to 40 minutes or until potatoes are tender and the top is golden brown and crusty.

Serves 4 to 6

Vegetable Goulash

Brimming over with flavour and soured cream, this is a simple vegetarian dish that teams superbly with boiled potatoes.

2 tablespoons salad oil
8 oz (225 g) onions, sliced thinly
1 garlic clove, sliced
8 oz (225 g) red or green peppers (or mixture), cut into strips
8 oz (225 g) marrow (weight after peeling and removing centre seeds), diced
6 oz (175 g) small carrots, thinly sliced
2 tablespoons salad oil
1 level tablespoon paprika
1 level tablespoon tomato purée
$\frac{1}{2}$ level teaspoon caraway seeds
2 level teaspoons light brown soft sugar
2 level teaspoons salt
$\frac{1}{4}$ pint (150 ml) tomato juice
5 oz (142 ml) carton soured cream

1. Heat oil in large pan. Add prepared vegetables. Fry, covered, for 15 minutes over medium heat, stirring twice.
2. Mix in paprika, purée, caraway seeds, sugar, salt and tomato juice. Bring to boil, stirring. Lower heat. Cover.
3. Simmer gently for about 30 to 40 minutes or until vegetables are tender. Stir in the soured cream and serve straight away.

Serves 4

Mediterranean Green Noodle Casserole

Colourful and unusual, this is one of my favourite non-meat pasta dishes.

4 oz (125 g) onions, chopped
2 oz (50 g) butter or margarine
6 oz (175 g) green ribbon noodles
14 oz (400 g) can tomatoes
8 oz (225 g) carton cottage cheese
salt and pepper
2 oz (50 g) Cheddar cheese, grated

Garnish
1 Grade 2 hard-boiled egg, cut into wedges
12 black olives

1. Fry onions gently in the butter or margarine until pale gold. Meanwhile, cook noodles until tender in plenty of boiling salted water as directed on the packet. Drain and return to pan in which they were cooked.
2. Add fried onions, tomatoes with liquid from can, and the cottage cheese. Season to taste with salt and pepper. Transfer to greased heatproof dish.
3. Sprinkle to with Cheddar cheese then reheat and brown for about 20 to 30 minutes in moderately hot oven set to 200°C (400°F), Gas 6.
4. Garnish with wedges of egg and the olives. Serve while still hot.

Serves 4

Dutch Vegetable Hotpot

If you remember to cook the potatoes one day ahead, you'll have a fast-to-prepare hotpot which makes a most pleasant spring and summer dish for those who fancy a meatless meal. For a change, try substituting celeriac for potatoes.

1½ lb (675 g) cold cooked potatoes, sliced thickly
1 lb (450 g) tomatoes, blanched, skinned and thickly sliced (try to use large Dutch ones)
1 bunch of spring onions, chopped
2 heaped tablespoons chopped parsley
8 oz (225 g) Gouda cheese, grated
salt and pepper
2 level tablespoons cornflour
2 tablespoons cold milk
¼ pint (150 ml) chicken stock or vegetable water
large pinch of grated nutmeg

1. Fill medium-sized greased casserole with alternate layers of potatoes and tomatoes, sprinkling onions, parsley, 4 oz (125 g) cheese and salt and pepper between the layers. Finish with a layer of potatoes.
2. Mix cornflour smoothly with milk. Mix in stock or vegetable water and the nutmeg. Pour carefully into dish. Sprinkle rest of cheese on top. Bake, uncovered, until golden, allowing about 30 to 40 minutes in moderate oven set to 180°C (350°F), Gas 4.

Serves 4

Risotto

A non-meat meal which stands on its own, this Italian dish is superbly creamy and fine-flavoured. It can also be served as an accompaniment to meat or chicken dishes.

2 teaspoons olive oil
3 oz (75 g) butter
3 oz (75 g) onions, chopped
12 oz (350 g) round grain pudding rice
2 pints (1¾ litres) chicken or vegetable stock
¼ pint (150 ml) dry white wine
salt and pepper
3 oz (75 g) grated Parmesan cheese

1. Heat the oil and half the butter in pan. Add onions. Fry until soft but still pale gold. Keep heat low and allow about 7 minutes.
2. Add rice. Fry gently for about 2 minutes. Gradually pour in stock over a period of 30 to 40 minutes, cooking and stirring gently all the time.
3. Continue to simmer, uncovered, for another 30 minutes or until mixture thickens and much of the liquid has evaporated. Stir frequently to prevent sticking.
4. Pour in wine. Simmer, uncovered, for another 15 to 20 minutes. Fork in rest of butter and all the cheese. Spoon on to warm plates. If liked, sprinkle extra grated Parmesan cheese over the top of each.

Serves 4 to 6

Exotic Peppers

Sustaining and healthy, these will appeal to all those who enjoy slightly exotic vegetable combinations which are neither too expensive nor too time-consuming to prepare.

> 8 medium peppers (1½ lb or 675 g)
> 3 tablespoons salad oil
> 8 oz (225 g) onions, chopped
> 8 oz (225 g) mushrooms with stalks, coarsely chopped
> 6 oz (175 g) tomatoes, blanched, skinned and chopped
> 6 oz (175 g) easy-cook long grain rice
> ¾ pint (375 ml) water
> 2 level teaspoons salt
> ½ pint (275 ml) tomato juice

1. Wash and dry peppers. Cut off tops and set aside for lids. Remove inside fibres and seeds from each and discard. If necessary, cut very thin slivers off the bases of peppers so that they stand upright without toppling.
2. Heat oil in pan. Add onions. Fry until light gold. Stir in mushrooms. Fry for 5 minutes. Mix in tomatoes, rice, water and salt.
3. Spoon rice mixture into peppers then stand upright, and close together, in saucepan. Top with reserved pepper lids.
4. Pour tomato juice into pan. Bring to boil. Lower heat and cover. Simmer gently for 45 minutes. Allow 2 peppers per person and coat with pan juices.

Serves 4

Gratin Dauphinoise

In the old tradition of haute cuisine, Gratin Dauphinoise always struck me as a marvellous main course lunch or supper dish, ideal with a gently tossed green salad and a well-cooled dryish white wine.

1 garlic clove
butter
2 lb (900 g) potatoes
12 oz (350 g) Gruyère cheese, grated
salt and pepper
¾ pint (425 ml) milk
¼ level teaspoon nutmeg
1½ oz (40 g) butter, melted
2 level tablespoons toasted breadcrumbs

1. Press cut clove of garlic against side of 3-pint (1¾-litre) shallow heatproof dish. Brush base and sides with melted butter.
2. Halve potatoes then cut into wafer thin slices either by slicing with knife, grating or feeding through food processor. Tip into teatowel and wring dry.
3. Fill dish with layers of potatoes and cheese, beginning and ending with potatoes and sprinkling salt and pepper between layers. Heat milk to boiling with nutmeg. Pour carefully into dish. Trickle butter over top then sprinkle with crumbs.
4. Bake for 45 to 55 minutes in moderately hot oven set to 200°C (400°F),Gas 6, when top layer should be golden brown and potatoes cooked through. If they still seem on the hard side, cover dish with foil to prevent top from over-browning and continue to cook for another 15 to 30 minutes.

Serves 4 to 6

Custard Dauphinoise Potatoes
Make as the Gratin Dauphinoise but beat hot (not boiling) milk with 2 Grade 3 eggs.

175

Mixed Vegetable and Cheese Casserole

A bountiful dish with a gloriously rich flavour. Bake potatoes in their jackets at the same time to serve with it.

2 bulbs (about 1 lb or 450 g) of Florence fennel
8 oz (225 g) carrots, thinly sliced
8 oz (225 g) onions, thinly sliced
8 oz (225 g) courgettes, thinly sliced
8 oz (225 g) broad beans, weighed after shelling
1 level teaspoon mixed herbs
1 can condensed cream of celery soup
½ pint (275 ml) boiling water
8 oz (225 g) Cheddar cheese, grated
salt and pepper
1 level teaspoon paprika
1 level teaspoon poppy seeds (optional)

1. Trim wispy ends off fennel but leave on the side shoots. Grate bulbs then tip into bowl. Add carrots, onions and courgettes with beans and herbs.
2. Mix soup and water gently together until smooth. Combine with vegetables and 5 oz (150 g) cheese.
3. Season to taste with salt and pepper then tip into deep, greased casserole. Cover with lid or greased foil then bake for 1¼ to 1½ hours in moderate oven set to 180°C (350°F), Gas 4 until vegetables are tender.
4. Uncover. Sprinkle rest of cheese on top then dust with paprika and poppy seeds. Brown under hot grill.

Serves 6

Vegetable and Cheese Nut Casserole
Make exactly as previous recipe but add 2 oz (50 g) lightly toasted unsalted cashews at same time as cheese.

Mushroom and Potato Braise

A very easy on-the-hob vegetarian braise based on mushrooms and potatoes, tastily flavoured with onions and nutmeg.

2 oz (50 g) butter or margarine
1 lb (450 g) potatoes, grated
2 oz (50 g) onion, grated
4 oz (125 g) carrots, sliced
¼ level teaspoon nutmeg
1 level teaspoon salt
freshly milled pepper to taste
1 can condensed cream of mushroom soup
¼ pint (150 ml) boiling water
1 lb (450 g) button mushrooms
6 oz (175 g) Cheddar cheese, grated

1. Heat butter or margarine in large saucepan. Add prepared vegetables.
2. Fry fairly briskly for 5 minutes, turning frequently. Season with nutmeg, salt and pepper. Leave over low heat.
3. Whisk soup and water well together. Add to pan with washed and trimmed mushrooms, left whole.
4. Mix well and slowly bring to boil, stirring. Lower heat. Cover. Simmer gently for 45 minutes, stirring occasionally.
5. Spoon on to plates and sprinkle thickly with cheese. Serve while still very hot.

Serves 4 to 6

Crispy Tomato Layer Bake

Well worth making in the summer when tomatoes are plentiful, and ideally suited to weekend brunch or a light supper.

4 large slices brown bread, with crusts left on
2 oz (50 g) butter or margarine
2 heaped tablespoons chopped parsley
1 garlic clove, crushed (optional)
2 lb (900 g) tomatoes, sliced
6 oz (175 g) Lancashire cheese, crumbled
1 level teaspoon mustard powder
salt and pepper

1. Crumb bread in blender or food processor. Heat butter or margarine in frying pan. Add crumbs, parsley and garlic if used.
2. Fry for about 10 minutes over low heat turning continuously until well-browned and crisp.
3. Fill a deep, buttered heatproof dish with alternate layers of tomatoes, fried crumb mixture, cheese and mustard. Sprinkle salt and pepper to taste between the layers.
4. End with a layer of cheese then bake, uncovered, for 40 to 45 minutes in a moderately hot oven set to 200°C (400°F), Gas 6.

Serves 4

Golden Leek and Potato Pie

An economical dish for mid-week eating which is also appetising and nourishing. If you prefer, substitute 12 oz (350 g) thinly sliced onions for the leeks. (See jacket picture.)

$1\frac{1}{4}$ lb (575 g) potatoes
1 lb (450 g) leeks, trimmed with 2 inches (5 cm) green 'skirt' left on
8 oz (225 g) Cheddar cheese, grated
2 oz (50 g) salted peanuts, finely chopped
salt and pepper
$\frac{1}{2}$ pint (275 ml) warm milk
4 tomatoes, sliced
chopped parsley to garnish

1. Very thinly slice potatoes and leave in bowl of cold water. Slit leeks and wash thoroughly under cold running water. Cut into thick slices.
2. Fill a deep, greased heatproof dish with alternate layers of well-drained potatoes, leeks, cheese and nuts. Sprinkle salt and pepper to taste between the layers. End with cheese and a sprinkling of nuts, then pour milk gently down side of dish.
3. Bake, uncovered, until potatoes are tender, allowing about $1\frac{1}{2}$ to $1\frac{3}{4}$ hours in a moderate oven set 180°C (350°F),Gas 4.
4. Place tomatoes around edge of casserole and return to oven for 5 to 7 minutes. Garnish with chopped parsley and serve.

Serves 4 to 6

Swiss Style Potato `Custard´

A two-part dish made with parboiled potatoes and Gruyère cheese. It is elegant and sophisticated, well-suited to lunch or supper, served with a salad.

1½ lb (675 g) peeled potatoes, halved
6 oz (175 g) Gruyère cheese, grated
2 heaped tablespoons finely chopped parsley
¼ pint (150 ml) single cream
2 Grade 2 eggs
1 level teaspoon continental mustard
1 to 1½ level teaspoons salt
1 garlic clove, crushed (optional)

1. Cook potatoes in boiling salted water for no more than 10 minutes. Drain and rinse under cold water. Slice.
2. Two-thirds fill a greased heatproof dish with alternate layers of potatoes, cheese and parsley. Begin with potatoes and end with cheese.
3. Beat together all remaining ingredients. Pour carefully down side of dish. Leave to stand for 20 minutes.
4. Bake, uncovered, until cooked through and golden, allowing about 40 to 45 minutes in moderate oven set to 180°C (350°F),Gas 4.

Serves 4

Ratatouille with Wine

A now familiar dish from the Mediterranean, I love Ratatouille simmered with French 'vin de pays' and spooned atop fluffy rice for a main course, lunch or supper dish.

  2 tablespoons salad oil
  6 oz (175 g) onions, thinly sliced
  2 garlic cloves, sliced
  1 lb (450 g) assorted coloured peppers, cut into strips
  1 lb (450 g) aubergines, unpeeled and sliced
  1 lb (450 g) courgettes, sliced
  14 oz (400 g) can tomatoes
  ¼ pint (150 ml) dry red wine
  1 level teaspoon Pizza seasoning herbs or marjoram or oregano
  1 to 2 level teaspoons salt
  freshly cooked rice
  3 heaped tablespoons chopped parsley

1. Heat oil in large pan. Add onions, garlic, pepper strips, aubergines and courgettes. Cover. Fry for 10 minutes over medium heat.
2. Stir in rest of ingredients. Simmer, half-covered, over a fairly low heat for about 2 hours or until most of the liquid has boiled away.
3. Spoon over servings of freshly cooked rice. Sprinkle with parsley.

Serves 8

Lamb Ratatouille
Follow the previous recipe but use rosé instead of red wine and fry 2 lb (900 g) cubed leg of lamb (no bone included in weight) with all the vegetables. Simmer, covered, for 2 hours. Stir occasionally.

Beef Ratatouille
Follow the recipe for Ratatouille with Wine but fry 2 lb (900 g) strips of braising steak with all the vegetables. Simmer, covered, for about 2 to 2½ hours, and serve with flat ribbon noodles.

181

Acknowledgements

American Rice Council
Breville Appliances
British Chicken
British Sausages
Brittany Fruit and Vegetables
Campbell's Soups
Carmel Produce
Central Bureau of Fruit and Vegetable Auctions in Holland
Colman Foods
Corningware
Crabtree & Evelyn
Danish Dairy Produce
Dutch Dairy Bureau
Elsenham
English Farmhouse Cheeses
Kitchen Devil Knives
Kraft Foods
Le Creuset
Pifco Appliances
Pyrex
Rank Hovis MacDougall
Russell Hobbs
Salton
Sharwoods Products
Spanish Olives
Sunbeam Appliances
Tefal
Tower Houseware

Index

184

185

186

187

190